The Victory Book

The Workbook That Will Take You Rapidly Out Of Debt!

Financial Freedom Series,

Volume III

The Victory Book

The Workbook That Will Take You Rapidly Out Of Debt!

Financial Freedom Series,

Volume III

By
John Avanzini & Patrick Ondrey

HIS Publishing Company
Hurst, Texas 76053

The Victory Book—
The Workbook That Will Take You Rapidly Out Of Debt!
Financial Freedom Series, Volume III

ISBN 1-878605-07-0

First Printing: 145,000 copies

HIS Publishing Company
P.O. Box 1096
Hurst, Texas 76053

To every pastor

throughout the world.

Our prayer is that **The Victory Book**

will be a tool in your hand

to help you bring forth

a debt-free congregation!

Contents

Foreword

For months you have heard John Avanzini talking about how Christians need to get out of debt. It is a truth that has been emphasized often on the Trinity Broadcasting Network. Many of you have read his books, *War On Debt* and *Rapid Debt-Reduction Strategies,* but you may still be wondering, "How do I actually go about getting out of debt?"

You will find the answer to that question in this, *The Victory Book*. This workbook takes the information from *War On Debt* and *Rapid Debt-Reduction Strategies* and puts it into a format you can easily follow. All you have to do is provide the commitment, and this book will provide the rest. Its simple, step-by-step method will not just show you how to live with debt, but it will show you how to totally get out of debt.

As most of you know, Jan and I are firm believers in staying out of debt, and we can confirm that the debt-free life is more pleasant than the debt-ridden life. We want you to experience the peace of this lifestyle, too. That is why we encourage you to follow *The Victory Book* through to completion.

However, there is an even greater purpose for becoming debt free. Think of how much more we will be able to do to share the gospel when the Body of Christ is no longer overburdened with debt! Never again will we have to say "no" because of the lack of funds.

Thank you for your faithfulness to TBN. It is our privilege to be partners with you in the War On Debt.

Paul Crouch
Founder and President
Trinity Broadcasting Network

Introduction

If we are to accurately measure victorious Christian living, we must evaluate it in more than one way. We determine one of the most important aspects of a victorious life by how well a person controls his finances.

As many Christians can attest, out-of-control spending puts victorious living beyond their reach. Invariably it will turn the joy of tithing and giving offerings into pressure instead of pleasure. Even though they know that without tithing the windows of heaven will close, they are tempted to skip this most necessary ordinance. Over-borrowing can shift their financial allegiance from God to the world. How true the Word of God is when it says:

> . . . the borrower is servant to the lender.
> **Proverbs 22:7**

Debt is a major obstacle that stands in the way of the financial freedom God has promised. Often it is caused by the Christian's own reluctance to submit his spending to the discipline of a Christ-centered budget. Lack of discipline causes the perpetual shortage he experiences, and keeps him from making any real progress toward the debt-free life God desires for him.

This Workbook Is Different

Before we go any further, we must point out the major differences between this workbook and others you may have seen. This is *The Victory Book!* Its purpose is not merely to organize your spending so that you can learn to live with your debt. Its purpose is to show you how to **rid yourself totally of debt,** once and for all. It will show you how to enter a **whole new lifestyle** — a debt-free lifestyle, to be exact. Within these pages, you will find simple, step-by-step procedures that will rapidly bring you completely out of debt. Add to that the **help of God,** and you have *The Victory Book,* not just another workbook. With it you will quickly attain the abundant finances you only wished for before.

Remember, **your God wants you out of debt.** He has made no secret of it. The Bible plainly shows us that He cancels the debts of His people.*

---

* *For instances of God's miraculous cancelation of debt, see* War On Debt, *Financial Freedom Series, Volume I. HIS Publishing Company, Hurst, TX 76053.*

Budget Is Not A Foul Word

Don't let the thought of organizing your financial matters become a stumbling block to you. You may tend to turn away from the term **budget** because of **the false concept** that a budget will somehow restrict you. The truth is that **a properly planned budget will liberate you.**

The Victory Book is not designed to limit your spending. It is designed to release your finances from the bondage that mismanagement has caused. Please realize that the limits you now experience in your spending were caused by your debt and your lack of proper planning. With the right budget, your debt will soon be gone, releasing most of your income to discretionary spending—that is, how you spend your income will be at your own discretion.

The Victory Book Will Put You In Control

Obtaining *The Victory Book* is your first bold step toward regaining control of your finances. We have specifically designed the forms in this book to put you **back in the driver's seat.** Prepare yourself, for there will be a few painful moments. They will not be caused by any drudgery this book brings. The pain will come as you realize just how foolish some of your past spending decisions have been. Do not let the thought of this discomfort discourage you from continuing. Once you have completed the forms, the pain will end and a new feeling of dominance will suddenly come over you. That feeling will **build your confidence** instead of tearing it down, and it will stay with you until Jesus comes.

Two Important Requirements

Let's not oversimplify. Success will require two important things of you. **First, your diligent attention to details** will be necessary. If you are not a detail person, do not let this throw you. We designed the work sheets to make it easy for you to keep control of the details.

Secondly, you must make a firm commitment to **follow through with the entire process** until its completion. Let's be honest with each other. We all know that simply filling out forms will not get you out of debt. It will take your diligence to complete all the required steps. Believe the word of those who have gone before you. If you provide the commitment, your effort will end in success.

We make you this solemn promise. **You will enjoy the debt-free life more than you are enjoying the debt-ridden life.** You have an opportunity to live in a new confidence that few Christians of our generation have known.

Based on God's Word

As it is with anything you plan to do with the help of God, it is necessary that you base your actions in the Word of God. Keep the following verse from the Bible in mind through your entire journey out of debt. **Let it be your scriptural basis of operation.**

For which of you, intending to build a tower, sitteth not down first, and counteth the cost, whether he have sufficient to finish it?
Luke 14:28

The Word of God clearly says that budgeting (planning ahead) is a Bible-approved method of approaching any problem. *The Victory Book* will help you count the cost and properly allocate your funds. In so doing, you will be in a perfect position **to get God's help** in your victorious march to a debt-free existence.

1

Smile — Your Future Looks Bright

When the present looks dull and unattractive, the child of God always has the privilege of looking ahead. Even if your past is filled with disappointment and your present is full of dark clouds, in Christ **the future can always be rosy.** Remember, as a Christian, you have the privilege of walking from glory unto glory, all the way into God's perfect day.

Jesus Looked To The Future

Do as our Lord did. When the ultimate horror of the crucifixion faced Him, Jesus lifted His head and **focused His attention** on the joyous day just beyond the cross.

> Looking unto Jesus the author and finisher of our faith; *who for the joy that was set before him* endured the cross. . . .
> **Hebrews 12:2**

Notice how His constant view of the future made it easier for Him to endure the pain and suffering of being crucified. In the same way, a look to the future will give you the strength to overcome the financial crisis you find yourself in today.

Keep in mind that it is God's nature to hold the best He has for us in reserve. At the wedding feast in Cana of Galilee, the best wine was not served first. It was saved for last.

> . . . the governor of the feast called the bridegroom,
> And saith unto him, Every man at the beginning doth set forth good wine; and when men have well drunk, then that which is worse; but thou hast kept the good wine until now.
> **John 2:9,10**

The debt nightmare you are presently experiencing does not have to be a permanent state. With the right attitude and commitment, it will soon be nothing more than an **unpleasant memory.** God will visit you just as he visited those at the wedding feast. He has saved something better for you. Say this to yourself, "God always saves the best for last. He will help me out of debt and into a better life."

Your Future Has Great Possibilities

Before we go any further, you need to have a good mental picture of what your debt-free future will be like. Think of a wonderful new **lifestyle of options** that will allow you to pick and choose instead of being bound to bland, predetermined decisions. Your new life will include the **vacations** you need. Your **children** will receive proper education. Your **automobile purchases** will be an enjoyment instead of the usual five-year debt sentence you have previously had to impose upon yourself. You will fund your **retirement** properly. **Tithes and offerings** will be a joyous interaction between you and your God.

You will have **no car payments, no mortgage payments, no past due notices.** Phone calls from bill collectors will be a thing of the past. Working overtime and weekends will be optional, not mandatory. You will be the **servant of God** instead of the servant of the lender.

. . . the borrower is servant to the lender.
Proverbs 22:7

The Following Is Not Optional

The following two sections are **extremely important,** for they will firmly fix in your mind what your life will be like when you are totally debt free. Don't short-change yourself by not fully completing them. You will be blessed and motivated as you see the goal for which you are striving.

Section A
Understanding The Road Ahead

Please answer the following questions.

1. We are regular tithers. _____ Yes _____ No
2. We give offerings regularly. _____ Yes _____ No
3. Our children will be college age in approximately _____ years.
4. That means we must set aside $_____ per year toward their education.
5. We have a college fund. _____ Yes _____ No
6. We plan to retire in _____ years
7. Our retirement/pension plan will pay $_____ per month at retirement.
8. This is a sufficient amount. _____ Yes _____ No
9. We make regular deposits into a savings account. _____ Yes _____ No
10. We will need to replace our automobile in approximately _____ years.

11. We are regularly setting aside money to purchase a new car when our present vehicle is worn out. _____ Yes _____ No
12. Our home will be paid off in _____ years.
13. We plan to be totally debt free in _____ years.
14. If we had extra money, we would buy the following necessities:

_____, _____, _____,

_____, _____, _____.

15. If we had extra money, we would give to the following ministries:

_____, _____, _____,

_____, _____, _____.

16. If we had extra money, we would buy the following luxuries:

_____, _____, _____,

_____, _____, _____.

Sometimes the Truth Hurts

Perhaps your finances are so far out of control that the previous questions actually hurt. If you are not able to give to God as He wants you to—if you have no savings account, no retirement plan, no college fund, no money set aside to replace your present automobile—if you have a thirty-year mortgage with no rapid debt-reduction strategy in place, **you are not in the minority.** You are actually one of the majority. That may not seem comforting, but take heart. Your financial circumstances will soon be much different.

Relief Is In Your Hands

The Victory Book you now hold in your hand will show you how to start making effective plans for those important future events. Not only will it lead you to answers for eliminating your present debt, but it will lead you to having plenty of money left over to give joyfully for any cause to which God directs you. However, to accomplish that lifestyle, you must set a specific goal—or better said, **you must have a vision.** For remember:

Where there is no vision, the people perish. . . .
Proverbs 29:18

Imagining a Debt-Free Life

One of the most important tools you will use in your war on debt is **your imagination.** The Bible says that as a man thinks in his heart, so is he (Proverbs 23:7). Almost anything you can imagine, you can accomplish.

You must begin to build a mental picture of yourself at the end of your out-of-debt campaign. Vividly visualize how your life will be when you are totally free from the clutches of debt. Imagine yourself writing out the final check for your mortgage. How will you and your family celebrate on that day?

Perhaps you will reward yourselves with **dinner at a special restaurant,** or maybe you will take that **dream vacation** your previous debt has denied you.

Complete this sentence: "When we are completely out of debt, we will celebrate by

_____

_____

_____ "

Make no mistake about it. Picturing the day you will be totally debt free is critical to the process of your getting out of debt. Make a habit of daily thinking pleasant thoughts about the times that lie beyond financial bondage.

Those who have been prisoners during wartime often report that they kept themselves alive by focusing their thoughts — not on their dismal circumstances, but on **how life would be when they were free.** Those who could not see beyond their prison walls often gave up before freedom came. Those who focused their attention on the days beyond captivity had a much greater survival rate.

Visualizing Is Scriptural

Please do not allow yourself to get hung up on the present-day teaching that all visualizing is part of the New Age Movement or that it somehow comes from the devil. Jesus Himself practiced visualizing future events. In Luke 10:18, when He said He **saw** (past tense) Satan as lightning falling, it would be hundreds of years before that event would actually happen in Revelation 12:9.

Remember, Jesus visualized the future to enable Him to endure the cross.

> **. . . who for the joy that was set before him endured the cross. . . .**
> **Hebrews 12:2**

Please notice that new agers and mystics, whose purpose is to accomplish their own will, misuse visualization. However, when Christian believers properly use it according to scriptural application, it is perfectly acceptable. Visualizing the future will help keep you moving toward your goal.

Section B
Your Dream Budget

To help you more easily picture your debt-free life, create a dream budget. List how you would spend your money if you had already paid off your bills. We have supplied you with an outline to help on the following page. Please don't limit yourself to our suggestions. Dream big, and remember. **If you can imagine it,** chances are **you will be able to accomplish it.**

Our Dream Budget

Item	Amt. Per Mo.
Tithe (10% of gross income)	
Offerings	
World Missions, Church Outreaches,	
Christian T.V. & Radio, Evangelists,	
The Poor, Etc.	
Withholding Tax	
Savings	
Normal Household Expenses	
Utilities, Maintenance	
Food	
Clothing	
Transportation	
Insurance	
Auto, Life, Health, Property/Casualty	
Gifts	
Christmas, Birthdays, Anniversaries	
Recreation/Entertainment	
Vacations, Hobbies	
Personal/Household	
Child Care	
Miscellaneous	
Mad Money	
Other	
Total Dream Budget	$

2
God Designed Your Spirit Man For Commitment

People ask us to make many commitments during a lifetime, but most folks do not really understand what a commitment is. A commitment is **a solemn promise or a pledge to something.** It is a state of being obligated.

Commitments take on many forms. You can commit yourself to a person, such as committing your life to Jesus Christ. You can commit yourself to a principle, such as getting out of debt.

Your successful journey into financial freedom will require **several firm commitments** from you. We will ask you to make some promises to yourself and to God. Please do not be afraid to do this. **God gets excited** when His sons and daughters make promises to Him. He loves to help those folks fulfill their commitments.

The Threefold Cord

You are not on your own in this venture. It is a joint effort. **God** is involved, **you** are involved, and **we** are involved. The Bible says it is hard to defeat three who are in agreement.

. . . a threefold cord is not quickly broken.
Ecclesiastes 4:12

The following sections will help prepare you for the commitment required to take you successfully to total freedom from debt. As you understand God's commitment to you and our commitment to support you in prayer, your will power will grow stronger, and you can be the overcomer God wants you to be.

Section A
Understanding What Commitment Is

As you answer the following questions, you will more fully understand your present level of commitment. We will then explain the level of commitment it will take for you to be successful in your war on debt. Please check the box that best expresses your answer.

25

1. How determined are you to become debt free?
☐ I don't really mind living with debt as long as I have enough money to pay the monthly bills.
☐ I want to get out of debt if it isn't too hard.
☐ I am determined to become debt free no matter what it takes.

2. Why do you want to be debt free?
☐ It sounds like a good idea.
☐ I want and need many things, but I have no room on my credit cards to buy them.
☐ I want to give more to the gospel than my debts allow me to give.

3. What do you think your chances are of soon being totally out of debt?
☐ I will probably never really be debt free.
☐ I will try and see what happens.
☐ With God's help, I know I will soon be totally debt free.

It's Time To Get Tough

A true commitment does not mean you will remain faithful only as long as the way is easy or pleasant. The commitment that overcomes debt is one that keeps on keeping on, no matter how difficult the task may become.

If the devil has his way, the months ahead will be a real struggle for you. Unless getting out of debt is more to you than just a good idea, you have little hope for success. However, if you are determined that **nothing will deter you** from your goal—that you will not allow deviations from the plan—then you will make it.

You can count on God's help if you make His purpose your own purpose. He wants you to have more than enough so that you can do your part in funding the great end-time harvest.

Section B
God's Commitment To You

The Bible contains God's written commitment to help you get out of debt. His Word clearly states that He wants His people free from financial bondage. God even provided a miracle of debt cancelation for His Son, Jesus.

In Matthew, the seventeenth chapter, the tax collector confronted Simon Peter. (Taxes are a bill, or debt, you owe.) Simon went into the house to get the money from the treasury, but Jesus stopped him from paying the bill in the usual manner. Instead

He sent him to the sea to catch a fish with a coin in its mouth. With that coin, our Lord's taxes were paid. **God miraculously canceled His Son's Debt!***

God is in favor of your getting out of debt, **even if He has to perform a miracle to accomplish it.** Think of it. The miracle of canceled debt probably awaits you in the near future — a miracle that will take you out of debt even more quickly than a budget can. However, keep in mind that God is more likely to perform the miracle of canceled debt for a person with an out-of-debt plan than He is for one who is aimlessly adrift in the sea of debt.

Read the following scripture out loud. Read it over and over again. Let it sink deep into your spirit. Remember, **you are not alone in this endeavor.**

> . . . He [God] hath said, I will never leave thee, nor forsake thee.
> **Hebrews 13:5**

Section C
Your Commitment To Become Debt Free

The first commitment you must make is that you will faithfully put into practice the things you learn in *The Victory Book*. Remember, it will do you no good if you only read what has been written. It will not help you to simply complete the work sheets, and then never look at them again. You must now commit yourself to **faithfully follow the instructions day in and day out until you have accomplished your goal.**

Say It Ten Times

Say the following sentence out loud ten times: "**I can** become debt free. **I can** become debt free. **I can** become debt free. **I can** become debt free. **I can** become debt free. **I can** become debt free. **I can** become debt free. **I can** become debt free. **I can** become debt free. **I can** become debt free."

If you still doubt that statement, simply ask yourself this question:

> **Is any thing too hard for the Lord? . . .**
> **Genesis 18:14**

_____

*   *For more information about how God canceled Jesus' debt, see chapter 10 of War On Debt, Financial Freedom Series, Volume I. HIS Publishing Company, Hurst, TX 76053.*

Of course, your answer is, "No! Nothing is too hard for my God — not even helping me get out of debt!"

Now say, "I can become debt free" ten more times. Just keep confessing it until you are convinced.

Something Is Beginning To Stir Within

The stirring you are beginning to feel inside is the Holy Spirit of God witnessing to you that financial freedom is soon to be a reality. Now you must begin to apply your faith, for without faith your task will be impossible to accomplish. When you are full of faith, you quickly become full of hope; and hope makes it easy to stick with a project, even when the going gets rough.

> **Now faith is the substance of things hoped for. . . .**
> **Hebrews 11:1**

You Are Not The First One

This ministry regularly receives testimonies from **people just like you** who have faithfully applied these principles to their lives. Many of them are already out of debt, and at this very moment, they are enjoying **life more abundantly.** This did not happen to them just because they faithfully paid their bills. It happened because **they made a specific commitment** to do something about getting out of debt. They asked God for guidance and started using God's Master Plan for quick debt payoff.

Do Not Be Double Minded

> **For let not that man think that he shall receive any thing of the Lord.**
> **A double minded man is unstable in all his ways.**
> **James 1:7,8**

Obligate yourself without reservation to this worthwhile task. Sign the following commitment with Holy Ghost conviction. Cut it out and mount it in a place where you will see it several times each day. Boldly give a copy to your pastor or ministry leader and ask him to agree with you in prayer. Clearly mark today's date on the calendar, for from this day forward, **you are on your way out of the land of debt** and into the reality of financial freedom!

Our Commitment To Become Debt Free

Be it known to all men and angels that we, the undersigned, resolve no longer to be satisfied with just getting by from paycheck to paycheck. From this day on, our primary financial objective is to eliminate every debt we have as quickly as we can. We uncompromisingly set our minds toward this goal.

We commit ourselves without reservation to thoroughly read and complete this workbook. We will answer every question and fill in every blank that pertains to our circumstances.

We are aware that it took time to get into debt, and it will take some time to get out of debt. However, we do not close our spirits to the miracle of total debt cancelation. No matter whether by miracle or by perseverance, we will be debt free!

Signature _____

Signature _____

Date _____

Our Commitment To Become Debt Free

Be it known to all men and angels that we, the undersigned, resolve no longer to be satisfied with just getting by from paycheck to paycheck. From this day on, our primary financial objective is to eliminate every debt we have as quickly as we can. We uncompromisingly set our minds toward this goal.

We commit ourselves without reservation to thoroughly read and complete this workbook. We will answer every question and fill in every blank that pertains to our circumstances.

We are aware that it took time to get into debt, and it will take some time to get out of debt. However, we do not close our spirits to the miracle of total debt cancelation. No matter whether by miracle or by perseverance, we will be debt free!

Signature _____

Signature _____

Date _____

Copy for Pastor or Ministry Leader

Section D
The Commitment Of This Ministry To You

Our part in helping you get out of debt is not just providing you with some good ideas. We have personally used the method explained in this book to come quickly and completely out of debt.* We are not practicing on you.

We want to stand with you. We want to pray for you all the way through your out-of-debt crusade. Just mail the following form to us, and we will return our signed commitment to stand with you in prayer by return mail. **Don't take this step lightly.** It is important to you, and it is important to us that we pray for you.

> **. . . The effectual fervent prayer of a righteous man availeth much.**
> **James 5:16**

How much more the prayers of two righteous men?

> **. . . two [shall] put ten thousand to flight. . . .**
> **Deuteronomy 32:30**

Together, we will make it! That's right! Together—**God, you, and our ministry.** You have become a part of a three-fold cord that will not be broken.

We are excited, God is excited, and by now, you are excited! So, **look out, devil!** Another of God's children is coming out of debt, **never to be caught in the debt trap again!**

---

*   *For the story of how John Avanzini paid off his debt, see chapters 3 and 4 of Rapid Debt-Reduction Strategies, Financial Freedom Series, Volume II. HIS Publishing Company, Hurst, TX 76053.*

This page is the form and the envelope. Complete the form, and fold where indicated. Use proper postage, and mail back to us.

Fold here

I have made a quality commitment to complete *The Victory Book*. Please agree with me in prayer for my success in getting out of debt. I will write to you and let you know when I have accomplished my goal.

(Please print clearly.)

Name:_____

Address:_____

City:_____State:_____Zip:_____

Fold here first.

John Avanzini & Patrick Ondrey
P.O. Box 1057
Hurst, TX 76053

Place
Proper
Postage
Here

3
You Must Operate Under An Open Heaven

How long will the Church continue to believe that there can be any financial blessings from God under a **closed heaven**? Malachi 3:10 clearly teaches us that only after faithful tithing begins do the windows of heaven open.

> **Bring ye all the tithes into the storehouse, that there may be meat in mine house, and prove me now herewith, saith the Lord of hosts, if I will not** *open you the windows of heaven,* **and pour you out a blessing. . . .**
> **Malachi 3:10**

Only A Few Tithe

With only about 18 percent of active church members tithing, it is no wonder the Church is so deeply in debt. Rampant debt is a common occurrence under a closed heaven. If you are not a regular tither, **it is important that you start tithing today.** If you choose to continue as a non-tither, neither our prayers nor *The Victory Book* will do you much good. There is little chance for victory unless you are obedient in the matter of tithing.

Try A Better Way

Haven't you tried it your way long enough? Let's now try it God's way.

> **For my thoughts are not your thoughts, neither are your ways my ways,** saith the Lord.
> **Isaiah 55:8**

In this chapter we will help you understand the tithe more fully as well as helping you make the commitment that is needed to begin tithing.

Section A
Understanding The Tithe

You may be asking, "How can I possibly afford to pay tithes? I am already up to my eyeballs in debt!"

We answer this question with a question. How will you ever get out of debt **unless you can get rid of the devourer?** God's only promise to rebuke the devourer is to those who tithe.

> **Bring ye all the tithes into the storehouse, that there may be meat in mine house, and prove me now herewith, saith the Lord of hosts, if I will not open you the windows of heaven . . . .**
> **And *I will rebuke the devourer for your sakes,* and he shall not destroy the fruits of your ground; neither shall your vine cast her fruit before the time in the field, saith the Lord of hosts.**
> **Malachi 3:10,11**

Remember, **disobedience** got you into financial trouble. So it stands to reason that **obedience** will get you out.

The following questions will help determine your understanding of the biblical principle of tithing. Please check what you feel is the correct answer. We will then explain the scriptural answers.

1. What is the tithe?
☐ It is a pledge.
☐ It is ten percent of all that I am increased.
☐ It is another word for an offering.

2. To whom does the tithe belong?
☐ To the person who works to earn it.
☐ To the pastor.
☐ To God.

3. What does tithing accomplish?
☐ It makes the preacher rich.
☐ It makes it harder for the tither to pay his bills.
☐ It opens the windows of heaven over the tither.

4. When does God pour out His blessings upon you?
☐ When you are faithful to tithe and give offerings.
☐ When you have a great need.
☐ When you earnestly pray.

Ten Percent Is The Lord's

The word **tithe** means "tenth." A tithe is ten percent of all you receive. It belongs to God alone (Leviticus 27:30). If you are not tithing, you are robbing God of that which rightfully belongs to Him (Malachi 3:8).

Consider this example. If you knew your next-door neighbors were stealing from you, would you be so foolish as to leave your windows open? Of course not. You would keep them closed and locked. In that same way, your God will not leave the windows of His heaven open over you if you are robbing Him of His tithe.

Tithing Benefits You

God wants you to have more than enough. Because of this, He has devised a plan that will provide for your every need. He is able to accomplish it through your faithfulness in tithes and offerings. It is sad to say, but far too few Christians ever experience the fullness of this plan. They foolishly struggle to keep up their payments to their creditors without even once giving a thought to their financial obligation to God.

Obedience Moves God

Do not let human reasoning confuse you. Your **need** will not open the windows of heaven. If God blessed people according to their needs, millions in India and Africa would not be starving. No matter how earnestly you may pray, it is only after you bring the tithe to God that He will pour out the blessings (Malachi 3:10). Remember, **no blessing can flow to those who choose to live under a closed heaven.**

Section B
Your Commitment To Tithe

Now that you fully understand how important tithing is to your financial success, obligate yourself to begin immediately. Boldly sign the commitment on the following page. **Give a copy to your pastor or ministry leader.** Prove God and see if He will not **open to you the windows of heaven and pour you out a great blessing.***

---

* *For further information on tithing, John Avanzini's cassette teaching tape, "Victory Under An Open Heaven," is available from HIS Publishing Company, Hurst, TX 76053*

Our Commitment To Tithe

This is to certify: that we, the undersigned, solemnly promise to begin tithing from this day forward.

We gratefully accept forgiveness from our God for not regularly tithing in the past. We promise to faithfully return to God 10 percent of all that He increases us from this day forward.

We are proving God, fully expecting that our tithe will open the windows of heaven over our lives and prepare us for God's blessings. By becoming faithful in tithing, we are believing that God will help us in our war on debt. We further believe He will send the miracle of canceled debt through the open windows of heaven.

Signature _____

Signature _____

Date _____

Our Commitment To Tithe

This is to certify that we, the undersigned, solemnly promise to begin tithing from this day forward

We gratefully accept forgiveness from our God for not regularly tithing in the past. We promise to faithfully return to God 10 percent of all that He increases us from this day forward

We are proving God, fully expecting that our tithe will open the windows of heaven over our lives and prepare us for God's blessings. By becoming faithful in tithing, we are believing that God will help us in our war on debt. We further believe He will send the miracle of canceled debt through the open windows of heaven.

_____ Signature

_____ Signature

_____ Date

Copy for Pastor or Ministry Leader

4
Knowing The Truth Will Set You Free

. . . ye shall know the truth, and the truth [you know] shall make you free.
John 8:32

If you do not know the whole truth about how you got into debt, you cannot be certain you won't end up in debt again. We designed this chapter to take you step by step into an understanding of how you got into your present financial bondage. It will also reveal the extent of your addiction to deficit spending (credit purchasing). Once that addiction becomes clear to you, it will be much easier to recognize and avoid the pitfalls that cause debt.

Carefully think out your answers. With them you should be able to discern the root of your problem. They will help you to identify the harmful behavior patterns that brought you into the trap of debt. Remember, **it is the truth you know** that will set you free.

Section A
Knowing How Your Debt Problem Developed

How did you get into such tremendous debt? Think about it for a few minutes. Then begin to write down in your own words what you feel happened. Pause a moment with each question here, and **try to remember the details.** Please don't fool yourself. Remember, **the biggest fool in town** is the one who **fools himself.**

When did you take out your first loan?_____

Which company sent you your first credit card?_____

Did you apply for that first card, or did it just come in the mail, even though you did not apply for it? _____ Applied _____ Came in Mail

Did credit cards cause you to desire to buy *things?* _____ Yes _____ No

Did credit cards cause you to start buying things immediately when you should have waited until later to buy them? _____ Yes _____ No

Perhaps your debt has diminished the quality of your family life, your marriage, or your business. List some specific areas of your life or the lives of your loved ones that your debt has adversely affected.

—————————, —————————, —————————,
—————————, —————————, —————————.

Circumstances beyond your control may have compounded your debt problem. You may have experienced a temporary loss of income. It could have been due to layoffs, a physical injury, or illness. List any uncontrollable circumstances that may have allowed debt to take over in your life.

—————————, —————————, —————————,
—————————, —————————, —————————.

Notice that when you are laboring under **a mountain of debt,** even the **slightest disruption** to your income becomes a major problem.

When did you make the purchase that you feel has caused you the greatest problem? _____

What was the item you purchased? _____

Under the same circumstances, would you purchase that item again if you had it all to do over again? _____ Yes _____ No

Think about the warning signs on the road to debt. Were there feelings of uneasiness? Did you start getting past-due notices? Did you start borrowing money to make payments on other bills? List any warning signs you bypassed or ignored.

_____

_____

Did you ever exaggerate your ability to repay when applying for a loan or credit card? If you did, explain those instances.

_____

_____

Did you ever spend extra money for certain credit cards (gold, platinum, etc.) simply for the prestige of owning such a credit-worthy symbol? If so, list the cards that fall into that category.

—————————, —————————, —————————.

Read back over your answers and see the patterns that led to your debt problem. It should be plain to see what happened.

Section B
Knowing Debt Is A Spirit

Without realizing it, you have come under the influence of the spirit of debt. Yes, you read right. There is a spirit of debt. At first it only nudged you into credit purchasing. Then, little by little, it gained control until now you are hopelessly locked into a lifestyle of debt. You know the spirit of debt has taken control when credit cards and time payments become your preferred way of purchasing, and your credit report becomes more important to you than your tithing report.

Driven To Buy On Credit

Folks who are under the control of the spirit of debt are no longer merely **nudged** to buy on credit. They are continually **driven** to go ever deeper into debt. When these people wake up and see what is happening to them, they often cannot believe they have borrowed so heavily. Many of them describe the whole experience as an **overpowering compulsion** to buy without any thought of how they will repay. Make no mistake about it. The spirit of debt is the primary culprit responsible for this kind of behavior.

If this sounds like you, do not despair. No matter how big your problem has become, God has the answer. You can change your behavior with the help of God.

I feel I am under the influence of the spirit of debt. _____ Yes _____ No

I want God to deliver me from the power of the spirit of debt. _____ Yes _____ No

Binding The Spirit

The Bible teaches us that all spirits are subject to the name of Jesus.

> **That at the name of Jesus *every knee should bow,* of things in heaven, and things in earth, and things under the earth.**
> **Philippians 2:10**

It is time for you to bind the spirit of debt. You must do it in the mighty name of Jesus. If you have not already done this, it is imperative that you do so before you go any further. As surely as His name has the power to **open blind eyes** and **heal crippled limbs,** it has the power to stop the influence of the spirit of debt in your life.*

Speak these words with conviction: **"In the name of Jesus,** I bind you Spirit of Debt. Take your hands off me. Loose me immediately, you foul spirit. Stop influencing my life! In Jesus' name, I command you to depart from me!"

Now that God has freed you from the devil's influence over your finances, you can proceed unhindered into your plan of rapid debt reduction.

Section C
Knowing The Extent Of Your Problem

Check the box that best expresses your answer. In some cases, more than one answer may pertain.

1. Most of my spending is done with:
☐ Credit cards.
☐ Cash.
☐ Checks.

2. When I use my credit cards:
☐ I never charge more than I can pay in full each month.
☐ I make only the minimum required payment each month.
☐ I keep my cards charged up to their limits.
☐ I sometimes borrow on one credit card to make payments on others.

3. I buy things I can't really afford:
☐ When I see a good sale.
☐ To cheer myself up.
☐ I don't buy things I can't afford.
☐ To keep up with my friends.

---

* *For further information on the spirit of debt, see chapter 13 of* **War On Debt,** *Financial Freedom Series, Volume I. HIS Publishing Company, Hurst, TX 76053.*

4. When I want something:
☐ I don't worry about how I will pay for it.
☐ I try to talk myself out of it, but it doesn't work.
☐ I carefully consider whether or not I can afford it.

5. When it comes to budgeting:
☐ I don't have a budget.
☐ I often spend money I set aside for other things on items I don't really need.
☐ I strictly follow my spending plan.

Responsible Action Is Necessary

What do your answers show about your spending patterns? Do you always think before you buy?

When you are issued a credit card, that does not mean you will be able to pay for anything and everything you charge. A credit card is like a checking account. Having one does not automatically mean you always have the available funds to cover any check you wish to write.

You are headed for trouble when you cannot afford to pay any more on your monthly credit card bills than the minimum payments. If you have no definite plan for paying off your credit cards, it will take many years and hundreds of dollars in interest to pay them in full. Wake up to the fact that if you continue to charge your credit cards to the limit, you will **never** pay them off.

From this day on, when you shop, your primary concern must no longer be whether or not an item is on sale. Neither can you any longer shop just to cheer yourself up or to keep up with the Joneses. From now on you must make responsible decisions about purchasing. Begin to use the following two rules for shopping.

First, do you really need the item you are tempted to buy? Secondly, do you have the extra money that it will cost? Just because you have a few dollars in the checking account does not mean you can safely spend them. **Don't forget about the mountain of bills you have coming due at the end of the month!**

You must create a workable budget and stick with it. Careful adherence to your plan will keep you from making the same mistakes over and over. We designed the following chapters of *The Victory Book* to lead you into the discipline it will take to accomplish that goal.

5

Getting Organized

Know ye not that they which run in a race run all, but one receiveth the prize? So run, that ye may obtain.

1 Corinthians 9:24

The Bible speaks of successfully running a race, but if you do not get off the starting blocks, you have no hope of winning. When it comes to declaring war on debt, the first step is knowing exactly where you are financially. Knowing the truth about your current position is the only way you can begin to make progress toward freedom from debt!

In this chapter, you will gather the information you need to create a plan of attack against your debt. You will position yourself for an effective start to the race.

Meet The Sample Family

Throughout the remainder of *The Victory Book,* we will be using The Sample Family as an example to help you understand how to complete the financial forms. We will call these forms "victory sheets," and we have provided two copies of each one for your convenience.

You will see that like many people, the Samples owe more than they can pay. Please understand that this family is not meant to represent **all** families. However, by using them as an example you will see, step by step, how they get out of debt. With that information you will also be able to get out of debt.

Section A
How Much You Owe

To properly determine exactly what you owe, you must complete the "How Much I Owe" victory sheet. Notice that you do not include normal, ongoing expenses such as food and utilities (unless you have charged these items). You include only debts that can be paid off once and for all such as loan payments, credit cards, and so on. **Do not include your home mortgage on this form.** We will deal with it separately in a later chapter.

Complete Your Form

On the following page you will find The Sample Family's "How Much I Owe" victory sheet. Please study it carefully. On your own "How Much I Owe" victory sheet, show the names of your lenders, your remaining balances, the minimum acceptable monthly payments, the interest rates, and the remaining number of payments. You should be able to find this information on your most recent statements. If they don't show the information you need, contact the lenders and ask for it.

Remember, it is important to list **every debt** you owe. Once you have completed this form, you will have finished the most painful portion of *The Victory Book*. You will be positioned in the starting blocks and ready to begin the race. **From that point on, the joy of becoming debt free will grow daily.**

The Sample Family

How Much I Owe

Name	Balance	Min. Pmt.	Interest	Mo. Left
Car	10,555	220	11%	48
Dept. Store #1	80	40	18%	2
Dept. Store #2	2,000	40	20%	50
Credit Union	3,000	210	12%	15
Visa #1	1,500	125	21%	12
Master Card	1,000	50	19%	20
Student Loan	200	30	4%	7
Visa #2	650	35	20%	19
Unsecured Note	700	125	14%	6
Orthodontist	1,000	100	0%	10
Finance Company	1,200	75	15%	16
Totals	$21,885	$1,050		

How Much I Owe

Name	Balance	Min. Pmt.	Interest	Mo. Left
Totals	$	$		

How Much I Owe

Name	Balance	Min. Pmt.	Interest	Mo. Left
Totals	$	$		

Section B
How Much You Earn

For some people, determining their total income is very easy. It is simply the gross amount (total before deductions are made) of their paycheck. Others have additional forms of income such as interest, dividends, rental income, child support or alimony, just to name a few. The important thing here is to include **all possible forms of income**. Not until you have listed all sources of income can you determine exactly how much you earn.

Calculating Your Income

You may receive your income once a week, twice a month, or monthly. The following calculations will show you how to determine your average monthly income:

♦ If you are paid weekly, multiply your weekly pay times 4.333.
♦ If you are paid bi-weekly, multiply your bi-weekly pay times 2.167.
♦ If you are paid semi-monthly, multiply your semi-monthly pay times 2.
♦ If you are paid monthly, your monthly pay equals your average monthly pay.
♦ If you are paid quarterly, divide your quarterly pay by 3.
♦ If you are paid annually, divide your annual pay by 12.

After reviewing The Sample Family example on the next page, complete your "Sources of Income" victory sheet. List the gross amount of each source and how often you receive it. Then use the "Average Monthly Income" victory sheet on that same page to determine your monthly income.

The Sample Family
Sources of Income

(Sources to consider: Employment, rental property, interest from savings accounts, dividends from stocks and bonds, partnership income, note payments to you, alimony, child support.)

Source	Amount	How Often
Mr. Sample's Job	1,800.00	Semi-mo.
Mrs. Sample's Job	215.00	Weekly
Child Support	150.00	Monthly
Dividend	25.50	Quarterly
Interest on Note	196.80	Annually
Partnership Income	135.44	Bi-weekly

Average Monthly Income

Item	Amount	× or ÷	=Per Mo.
Mr. Sample's Job	1,800.00	×2	3,600.00
Mrs. Sample's Job	215.00	×4.333	931.60
Child Support	150.00	×1	150.00
Dividend	25.50	÷3	8.50
Interest on Note	196.80	÷12	16.40
Partnership Income	135.44	×2.167	293.50
Total Average Monthly Income			$5,000.00

Sources of Income

(Sources to consider: Employment, rental property, interest from savings accounts, dividends from stocks and bonds, partnership income, note payments to you, alimony, child support.)

Source	Amount	How Often

Average Monthly Income

Item	Amount	× or ÷	=Per Mo.
Total Average Monthly Income			$

Sources of Income

(Sources to consider: Employment, rental property, interest from savings accounts, dividends from stocks and bonds, partnership income, note payments to you, alimony, child support.)

Source	Amount	How Often

Average Monthly Income

Item	Amount	× or ÷	=Per Mo.
Total Average Monthly Income			$

Section C
Your Actual Expenses

On the next page, carefully list your actual monthly expenses. Be as accurate as possible. Remember, this is the place where most people fall short. It is important that you list **all your expenses**. Missing even one will flaw your out-of-debt plan and will cause you to suffer a setback. (Just list the bills themselves at this time. You do not need to list the dollar amount.) **Do not include the items from your "How Much I Owe" victory sheet.**

After you have made your list on the "List of Expenses" victory sheet, compare it to the list of "Possible Expenses" which follows it. Some of the items you have overlooked may surprise you.

If you find you have left certain items off your own list, please add them. Keep in mind that we have listed as many possible expenses as we can, but there are still others. Don't be limited by our suggestions, for you may have expenses we have not listed.

List of Expenses

1. _____ 2 _____

3. _____ 4 _____

5. _____ 6. _____

7. _____ 8. _____

9. _____ 10. _____

11. _____ 12 _____

13. _____ 14 _____

15. _____ 16. _____

17. _____ 18 _____

19. _____ 20. _____

21. _____ 22. _____

23. _____ 24. _____

25. _____ 26 _____

27. _____ 28 _____

29. _____ 30 _____

31. _____ 32 _____

33. _____ 34. _____

35. _____ 36 _____

37. _____ 38. _____

39. _____ 40. _____

List of Expenses

1. _____   2 _____
3. _____   4 _____
5. _____   6. _____
7. _____   8. _____
9. _____   10. _____
11. _____   12 _____
13. _____   14 _____
15. _____   16. _____
17. _____   18 _____
19. _____   20. _____
21. _____   22. _____
23. _____   24. _____
25. _____   26 _____
27. _____   28 _____
29. _____   30 _____
31. _____   32 _____
33. _____   34. _____
35. _____   36 _____
37. _____   38. _____
39. _____   40. _____

Possible Expenses

A. Housing (25%)
Mortgage Payment
Rent
Electricity
Water
Gas
Heating Oil
Telephone
Cable T.V.
Maintenance
Ground Care
Property Tax
Other

B. Food (10%)
Groceries
Business Lunches
Other

C. Clothing (5%)
Adult
Children
Laundry/Dry Cleaning
Other

D. Medical (3%)
Medicine/Drugs
Dental
Eyeglasses
Doctor
Medical Insurance
Dental Insurance
Hospital
Other

E. Transportation (4%)
Registration
Gasoline
Oil/Antifreeze, etc.
Tires
Repairs
Inspection
Parking
Public Transportation
Other

F. Gifts & Donations (12%)
Church
Charities
Birthdays
Anniversaries
Business Related
Wedding/Baby
Other

G. Recreation/Entertainment (2%)
Vacations
Shows/Movies
Sporting Events
Dining
Clubs
Parties
Hobbies
Other

H. Personal/Household (4%)
Furniture
Kitchen Appliances
Utility Appliances
Electronic Appliances
Linens
Utensils
Tools
Beauty Shop & Supplies
Barber Shop & Supplies
Fingernails
Fitness Center
Toiletries
Reading Material
Pets & Supplies
Veterinarian
Other

I. Insurance (4%)
Auto
Life
Property/Casualty
Renter
Other

J. Withholding Taxes (22%)
Income (Federal)
Income (State)
Social Security (FICA)
Other

K. Support/Child Care (5%)
Alimony
Child Support
Day Care
Baby Sitting
Parents
Children's Allowances
Other

L. Savings (2%)
Regular
Seasonal
Retirement
Investment
College
Other

M. Miscellaneous (2%)
Christian/Private School Tuition
School Supplies
School Dorms
Athletic Fees
Union Dues
Professional Fees
Licenses
Lessons
Other

Section D
Your Reserve Expenses

Budget problems can also arise when people forget to set aside money each month for their reserve expenses. The term "reserve expenses" refers to those payments that do not come due every month. They may be payable quarterly, every six months, once a year, etc. If you do not set aside the money in reserve, you may spend it on other things.

Review The Sample Family "Reserve Expenses" victory sheet on the following page. Then take special note of those items on your expense list that are not due every month. Write them on your "Reserve Expenses" victory sheet. At the bottom of the form you will see how much you should set aside each month for these periodic payments.

Please note: Every three months you should update the "Reserve Expenses" victory sheet to be sure you have accounted for additions or deletions, as well as any change in dollars due. For that purpose, we have included enough copies for one year.

Section D
Your Reserve Expenses

The Sample Family
Reserve Expenses
1st Quarter

(Items to consider: Insurance, taxes, heating oil, clothing, vacations, dues, school expenses, gifts, medical expenses.)

Item	Due When	Amount	*Yearly Multiplier	Yearly Amt. Due	Divided By 12	Monthly Reserve
Household Maint.	Anly	636.00	×1	636.00	÷ 12	53.00
Property Tax	Anly	1,176.00	×1	1,176.00	÷ 12	98.00
Clothing	Anly	1,000.00	×1	1,000.00	÷ 12	83.33
Doctor Exams	Anly	300.00	×1	300.00	÷ 12	25.00
Prescriptions	Qtly	27.00	×4	108.00	÷ 12	9.00
Tires (2 per yr.)	Anly	140.00	×1	140.00	÷ 12	11.67
Car Registration	Anly	99.60	×1	99.60	÷ 12	8.30
Car Inspection	Anly	15.00	×1	15.00	÷ 12	1.25
Car Maintenance	Anly	300.00	×1	300.00	÷ 12	25.00
Christmas Gifts	Anly	1,000.00	×1	1,000.00	÷ 12	83.33
Birthday Gifts	Anly	200.00	×1	200.00	÷ 12	16.66
Anniversary Gifts	Anly	100.00	×1	100.00	÷ 12	8.33
Vacation	Anly	600.00	×1	600.00	÷ 12	50.00
Beauty Shop	S-Anly	60.00	×2	120.00	÷ 12	10.00
Veterinarian	Anly	100.00	×1	100.00	÷ 12	8.33
Auto Insurance	Qtly	249.90	×4	999.60	÷ 12	83.30
Christian School	Anly	4,200.00	×1	4,200.00	÷ 12	350.00
Soccer Club	S-Anly	198.00	×2	396.00	÷ 12	33.00
			×		÷ 12	
			×		÷ 12	
			×		÷ 12	
			×		÷ 12	
			×		÷ 12	
			×		÷ 12	
			×		÷ 12	
			×		÷ 12	
			×		÷ 12	
			×		÷ 12	
			×		÷ 12	
			Total Monthly Reserve			$957.50

*If due quarterly, multiply by 4
If due semi-annually, multiply by 2
If due annually, multiply by 1

Reserve Expenses
1st Quarter

(Items to consider: Insurance, taxes, heating oil, clothing, vacations, dues, school expenses, gifts, medical expenses.)

Item	Due When	Amount	*Yearly Multiplier	Yearly Amt. Due	Divided By 12	Monthly Reserve
			×		÷ 12	
			×		÷ 12	
			×		÷ 12	
			×		÷ 12	
			×		÷ 12	
			×		÷ 12	
			×		÷ 12	
			×		÷ 12	
			×		÷ 12	
			×		÷ 12	
			×		÷ 12	
			×		÷ 12	
			×		÷ 12	
			×		÷ 12	
			×		÷ 12	
			×		÷ 12	
			×		÷ 12	
			×		÷ 12	
			×		÷ 12	
			×		÷ 12	
			×		÷ 12	
			×		÷ 12	
			×		÷ 12	
			×		÷ 12	
			×		÷ 12	
			×		÷ 12	
			×		÷ 12	
			×		÷ 12	
			×		÷ 12	
			×		÷ 12	
			×		÷ 12	
				Total Monthly Reserve		$

*If due quarterly, multiply by 4
If due semi-annually, multiply by 2
If due annually, multiply by 1

Reserve Expenses
1st Quarter

(Items to consider: Insurance, taxes, heating oil, clothing, vacations, dues, school expenses, gifts, medical expenses.)

Item	Due When	Amount	*Yearly Multiplier	Yearly Amt. Due	Divided By 12	Monthly Reserve
			×		÷ 12	
			×		÷ 12	
			×		÷ 12	
			×		÷ 12	
			×		÷ 12	
			×		÷ 12	
			×		÷ 12	
			×		÷ 12	
			×		÷ 12	
			×		÷ 12	
			×		÷ 12	
			×		÷ 12	
			×		÷ 12	
			×		÷ 12	
			×		÷ 12	
			×		÷ 12	
			×		÷ 12	
			×		÷ 12	
			×		÷ 12	
			×		÷ 12	
			×		÷ 12	
			×		÷ 12	
			×		÷ 12	
			×		÷ 12	
			×		÷ 12	
			×		÷ 12	
			×		÷ 12	
			×		÷ 12	

Total Monthly Reserve $

*If due quarterly, multiply by 4
If due semi-annually, multiply by 2
If due annually, multiply by 1

Reserve Expenses
2nd Quarter

(Items to consider: Insurance, taxes, heating oil, clothing, vacations, dues, school expenses, gifts, medical expenses.)

Item	Due When	Amount	*Yearly Multiplier	Yearly Amt. Due	Divided By 12	Monthly Reserve
			×		÷ 12	
			×		÷ 12	
			×		÷ 12	
			×		÷ 12	
			×		÷ 12	
			×		÷ 12	
			×		÷ 12	
			×		÷ 12	
			×		÷ 12	
			×		÷ 12	
			×		÷ 12	
			×		÷ 12	
			×		÷ 12	
			×		÷ 12	
			×		÷ 12	
			×		÷ 12	
			×		÷ 12	
			×		÷ 12	
			×		÷ 12	
			×		÷ 12	
			×		÷ 12	
			×		÷ 12	
			×		÷ 12	
			×		÷ 12	
			×		÷ 12	
			×		÷ 12	
			×		÷ 12	
			×		÷ 12	
			×		÷ 12	
			×		÷ 12	
			×		÷ 12	
				Total Monthly Reserve		$

*If due quarterly, multiply by 4
If due semi-annually, multiply by 2
If due annually, multiply by 1

Reserve Expenses
2nd Quarter

(Items to consider: Insurance, taxes, heating oil, clothing, vacations, dues, school expenses, gifts, medical expenses.)

Item	Due When	Amount	*Yearly Multiplier	Yearly Amt. Due	Divided By 12	Monthly Reserve
			×		÷ 12	
			×		÷ 12	
			×		÷ 12	
			×		÷ 12	
			×		÷ 12	
			×		÷ 12	
			×		÷ 12	
			×		÷ 12	
			×		÷ 12	
			×		÷ 12	
			×		÷ 12	
			×		÷ 12	
			×		÷ 12	
			×		÷ 12	
			×		÷ 12	
			×		÷ 12	
			×		÷ 12	
			×		÷ 12	
			×		÷ 12	
			×		÷ 12	
			×		÷ 12	
			×		÷ 12	
			×		÷ 12	
			×		÷ 12	
			×		÷ 12	
			×		÷ 12	
			×		÷ 12	
			×		÷ 12	
			×		÷ 12	
					Total Monthly Reserve	$

*If due quarterly, multiply by 4
If due semi-annually, multiply by 2
If due annually, multiply by 1

Reserve Expenses
3rd Quarter

(Items to consider: Insurance, taxes, heating oil, clothing, vacations, dues, school expenses, gifts, medical expenses.)

Item	Due When	Amount	*Yearly Multiplier	Yearly Amt. Due	Divided By 12	Monthly Reserve
			×		÷ 12	
			×		÷ 12	
			×		÷ 12	
			×		÷ 12	
			×		÷ 12	
			×		÷ 12	
			×		÷ 12	
			×		÷ 12	
			×		÷ 12	
			×		÷ 12	
			×		÷ 12	
			×		÷ 12	
			×		÷ 12	
			×		÷ 12	
			×		÷ 12	
			×		÷ 12	
			×		÷ 12	
			×		÷ 12	
			×		÷ 12	
			×		÷ 12	
			×		÷ 12	
			×		÷ 12	
			×		÷ 12	
			×		÷ 12	
			×		÷ 12	
			×		÷ 12	
			×		÷ 12	
			×		÷ 12	
			×		÷ 12	
			×		÷ 12	
				Total Monthly Reserve		$

*If due quarterly, multiply by 4
If due semi-annually, multiply by 2
If due annually, multiply by 1

Reserve Expenses
3rd Quarter

(Items to consider: Insurance, taxes, heating oil, clothing, vacations, dues, school expenses, gifts, medical expenses.)

Item	Due When	Amount	*Yearly Multiplier	Yearly Amt. Due	Divided By 12	Monthly Reserve
			×		÷ 12	
			×		÷ 12	
			×		÷ 12	
			×		÷ 12	
			×		÷ 12	
			×		÷ 12	
			×		÷ 12	
			×		÷ 12	
			×		÷ 12	
			×		÷ 12	
			×		÷ 12	
			×		÷ 12	
			×		÷ 12	
			×		÷ 12	
			×		÷ 12	
			×		÷ 12	
			×		÷ 12	
			×		÷ 12	
			×		÷ 12	
			×		÷ 12	
			×		÷ 12	
			×		÷ 12	
			×		÷ 12	
			×		÷ 12	
			×		÷ 12	
			×		÷ 12	
			×		÷ 12	
			×		÷ 12	
			×		÷ 12	
			Total Monthly Reserve			$

*If due quarterly, multiply by 4
If due semi-annually, multiply by 2
If due annually, multiply by 1

Reserve Expenses
4th Quarter

(Items to consider: Insurance, taxes, heating oil, clothing, vacations, dues, school expenses, gifts, medical expenses.)

Item	Due When	Amount	*Yearly Multiplier	Yearly Amt. Due	Divided By 12	Monthly Reserve
			×		÷ 12	
			×		÷ 12	
			×		÷ 12	
			×		÷ 12	
			×		÷ 12	
			×		÷ 12	
			×		÷ 12	
			×		÷ 12	
			×		÷ 12	
			×		÷ 12	
			×		÷ 12	
			×		÷ 12	
			×		÷ 12	
			×		÷ 12	
			×		÷ 12	
			×		÷ 12	
			×		÷ 12	
			×		÷ 12	
			×		÷ 12	
			×		÷ 12	
			×		÷ 12	
			×		÷ 12	
			×		÷ 12	
			×		÷ 12	
			×		÷ 12	
			×		÷ 12	
			×		÷ 12	
			×		÷ 12	
			×		÷ 12	
			×		÷ 12	
				Total Monthly Reserve		$

*If due quarterly, multiply by 4
If due semi-annually, multiply by 2
If due annually, multiply by 1

Reserve Expenses
4th Quarter

(Items to consider: Insurance, taxes, heating oil, clothing, vacations, dues, school expenses, gifts, medical expenses.)

Item	Due When	Amount	*Yearly Multiplier	Yearly Amt. Due	Divided By 12	Monthly Reserve
			×		÷ 12	
			×		÷ 12	
			×		÷ 12	
			×		÷ 12	
			×		÷ 12	
			×		÷ 12	
			×		÷ 12	
			×		÷ 12	
			×		÷ 12	
			×		÷ 12	
			×		÷ 12	
			×		÷ 12	
			×		÷ 12	
			×		÷ 12	
			×		÷ 12	
			×		÷ 12	
			×		÷ 12	
			×		÷ 12	
			×		÷ 12	
			×		÷ 12	
			×		÷ 12	
			×		÷ 12	
			×		÷ 12	
			×		÷ 12	
			×		÷ 12	
			×		÷ 12	
			×		÷ 12	
			×		÷ 12	
			×		÷ 12	
			×		÷ 12	

Total Monthly Reserve $

*If due quarterly, multiply by 4
If due semi-annually, multiply by 2
If due annually, multiply by 1

Section E
Do Ends Meet?

Now that you have completed your expense list and determined your reserve account items, it is time to examine your cash flow position. By this we simply mean, do ends meet?

List each expense item again, but this time include the amount of the monthly payment. Also show the monthly reserve expense amounts you must set aside. We have provided the following "Monthly Expenses #1" victory sheet for this purpose. Remember, it is necessary to list **every item you owe** on this one — including your home mortgage.

To determine the proper category of each expense, look at the "Possible Expenses" list again, page 67. You will see that each category begins with a letter code. Place the proper letter code in the category column to indicate the category for each of your expenses. You will refer to this letter code in a later chapter.

At the end of your "Monthly Expenses #1" form, you will also list the total from your "How Much I Owe" victory sheet, page 55. There is no category letter for that total.

Average Monthly Cost

Some items, such as utilities, vary in cost from month to month. For instance, electric bills may be higher in summer due to air conditioning costs. Gas bills may be higher in winter due to heating costs.

To determine the monthly amount to use for this type of bill, total the charges for the past twelve-month period. Divide that amount by twelve. That will give you an average monthly cost. Please note that your monthly bill may be more or less than the average during any given month. If a bill is less than the average during one month, **do not spend the surplus.** Set the extra amount aside with your reserve dollars for the months that will cost more than the average payment.

Review the Sample family example on the following page. Then complete your own "Monthly Expenses #1" victory sheet.

The Sample Family Monthly Expenses #1

Item	Amt. Per Mo.	Category*
Tithes	500.00	F
Offerings	50.00	F
Withholding Tax	495.00	J
Social Security	240.00	J
Mortgage	850.00	A
Groceries	500.00	B
Electricity	75.00	A
Water	50.00	A
Gas	62.50	A
Telephone	45.00	A
Christian School Registration & Tuition	350.00	M
School Clothes	83.33	C
Prescriptions	9.00	D
Doctor Exams	25.00	D
Dental Insurance	30.00	D
Gasoline	80.00	E
Tires	11.67	E
Car Registration	8.30	E
Car Inspection	1.25	E
Christmas Gifts	83.33	F
Birthday Gifts	16.66	F
Anniversary Gifts	8.33	F
Vacation	50.00	G
Movies	35.00	G
Dining Out	130.00	G
Barber	30.00	H
Beauty Shop	10.00	H
Toiletries	25.00	H
Veterinarian	8.33	H
Dog Food	10.00	H
Car Insurance	83.30	I
Life Insurance	35.00	I
Soccer Club	33.00	M
Car Maintenance	25.00	E
Property Tax	98.00	A
Household Maintenance	53.00	A
Total mo. pmts. from **"How Much I Owe"** sheet	1,050.00	
Total Monthly Expenses	$5,250.00	

From "Possible Expenses," page 67

Monthly Expenses #1

Item	Amt. Per Mo.	Category
Total mo. pmts. from **"How Much I Owe"** sheet		
Total Monthly Expenses	$	

Monthly Expenses #1

Item	Amt. Per Mo.	Category
Total mo. pmts. from **"How Much I Owe"** sheet		
Total Monthly Expenses	$	

The Sample Family Is Overspent

You will quickly notice that The Sample Family's monthly expenses are $250 more than their income every month.

The Sample Family Monthly Income	$ 5,000.00
The Sample Family Monthly Expenses	– 5,250.00
Difference	- 250.00

Are You Overspent?

Compare your total from the preceding "Monthly Expenses #1" victory sheet to your total on the "Average Monthly Income" victory sheet on page 61. What do you find?

Total Monthly Income   _____

Total Monthly Expense   = _____

Difference (+ or -)   _____

My total monthly expenses are:

☐ more than my monthly income.
☐ less than my monthly income.
☐ the same as my monthly income.

You have now accomplished what most people feel is the hardest portion of this process—**facing the truth.** If the picture looks bleak, and you feel you are hopelessly falling behind in the race, you may be tempted to give up, **but don't you dare even think that thought!** Now that you have faced the facts, you have finally reached a position where you can do something constructive about your debt problem.

It is now time for you to be commended. Fill in your name and the date on the following certificate and put it in a place where you will look at it often.

Certificate of Accomplishment

Research and Calculation

Congratulations are in order for _____ !

You have successfully completed the major obstacle that stood in the way of financial freedom. You have listed and organized your debts.

A significant part of your out-of-debt journey is now behind you. Keep up the good work!

John Avanzini

Patrick Ondrey

Date _____

6

Spiritual Strength And Motivation

You are no longer at square one. You have faced your problem and have begun constructive change. Consider for a moment what you have really done. By organizing and listing your bills, you have started your **war on debt.**

There is an expression you should understand before going any further — **behavior modification.** While it is primarily a secular term, it actually expresses the results of a valid biblical principle. God calls that principle the "renewing of your mind."

> ... be not conformed to this world: *but be ye transformed by the renewing of your mind....*
> **Romans 12:2**

The renewing of your mind is accomplished through your understanding of the Scripture. Don't become weary with the many biblical references we use in this chapter, for you must be a **hearer** of God's Word before you can become an effective **doer** of it. **Hear** what the Bible says about money, and it will cause your faith for finances to grow. Remember:

> ... faith cometh *by hearing,* and hearing *by the word of God.*
> **Romans 10:17**

Winning your war on debt will require **faith** strong enough to bring about the behavior changes you are seeking. Be encouraged, for the very **hope** you have of overcoming debt is a sign that your faith is alive and well.

> Now *faith* is the *substance* of things *hoped for....*
> **Hebrews 11:1**

The more you trust God in faith for deliverance from debt, the sooner you will realize your goal. The stronger the Word of God becomes in you, the easier it will be to modify your behavior. With a renewed mind, your **spending habits** will quickly begin to change, and your **giving patterns** will come into line with God's will.

God's Way Is The Fastest Way

Becoming a doer of the Word will expedite your financial freedom. Everything moves more smoothly when you get into the flow with God. The more you realize that

God desires to help you out of debt, the sooner the anxiety (worry) over your debt dilemma will end. Remember this unchanging truth. **As long as you live in debt, you will be under the pressure of debt.** When debt begins to go, pressure will also go, and joyful living will become your portion.

You Want To Change

Your will always plays a major part in every victory you experience. Victory in salvation did not take place until your will came in line with God's will. You did not follow Jesus in baptism until your will joined with God's will. You were quickly filled with the Holy Spirit when your will began to flow with His will.

In exactly that same way, your willingness to change (modify your behavior) makes your goal of debt freedom easier to accomplish. The very fact that you have made it this far in *The Victory Book* proves that you are **willing to change.**

Say What You Intend To Do

Now, begin to clearly **speak that you have changed** the way you handle your finances. As often as you can, you must say that you have stopped **deficit spending.** Say it loud and say it often. Tell everyone you will soon be totally debt free. Say out loud, right now, **"I am just a few months from being totally debt free!"**

Didn't that sound good? Don't think it was unscriptural, for the Bible says:

> . . . whosoever shall *say* . . . and *shall not doubt* . . . but shall *believe.* . . shall have *whatsoever he saith.*
>
> **Mark 11:23**

Saying you are going to do a thing is a big step toward doing it. Remember, God's Word says **you will have whatever you say.**

Study The Word Of God

Regular reading and study of the Bible will be especially important during the following months. The value of studying the Bible is plainly stated:

> **This book of the law shall not depart out of thy mouth; but thou shalt meditate therein day and night, that thou mayest observe to do according to all that is written therein:** *for then thou shalt make thy way prosperous, and then thou shalt have good success.*
>
> **Joshua 1:8**

If you will speak, study, and do the Word of God, He promises to lead you into a **profitable lifestyle.**

> **Thus saith the Lord, thy Redeemer, the Holy One of Israel; I am the Lord thy God *which teacheth thee to profit*, which leadeth thee by the way that thou shouldest go.**
> **Isaiah 48:17**

God wants you to profit. He does not want past-due bills and insufficiency to burden you down. He literally wants you to have more than enough!

> **Let them shout for joy, and be glad, that favour my righteous cause: yea, let them say continually, Let the Lord be magnified, *which hath pleasure in the prosperity of his servant*.**
> **Psalm 35:27**

God's way of prospering will not cause you any sorrow.

> **The blessing of the Lord, *it maketh rich*, and *he addeth no sorrow with it*.**
> **Proverbs 10:22**

God gladly provides the everyday things you need.

> **According as his divine power hath *given unto us all things that pertain unto life* and godliness, through the knowledge of him that hath called us to glory and virtue.**
> **2 Peter 1:3**

Jesus came to give you abundant life. That means life with all your bills paid in full!

> **. . . I am come that they might have *life*, and that they might have it *more abundantly*.**
> **John 10:10**

The Word of God says you can overcome the world's system of debt.

> **For whatsoever is born of God *overcometh the world:* and this is the victory that overcometh the world, *even our faith*.**
> **1 John 5:4**

With your strong faith, you will please God.

> **. . . without faith it is impossible to please him. . . .**
> **Hebrews 11:6**

If you please God, nothing can stand against you.

> **. . . If God be for us, who can be against us?**
> **Romans 8:31**

With faith, getting out of debt becomes possible.

> **. . . all things are possible to him that believeth.**
> **Mark 9:23**

Remember, your faith draws God's answer to you.

> **. . . According to your faith be it unto you.**
> **Matthew 9:29**

As you learn God's Word about your victory and begin to act upon it in faith, **your financial difficulties will crumble before you.** The further you go, the more confident you will become that **God will see you through.** You will gain the second wind you need to start sprinting to the end of the race.

Fill in the following blanks to be certain that the motivation of this chapter is firmly planted in your spirit. **Review this chapter whenever you need encouragement.**

1. What secular term actually expresses the results of a valid biblical principle? _____ _____
2. God calls behavior modification the "renewing of _____ _____."
3. ". . . be not conformed to this world: but be ye_____ by the _____ of your mind. . . ." Romans 12:2
4. You must be a **hearer** of God's Word before you can become an effective _____ of it.
5. ". . . faith cometh by _____ and hearing by the _____ of God." Romans 10:17
6. "Now faith is the substance of things _____ for. . . ." Hebrews 11:1
7. The stronger the Word of God becomes in you, the easier it will be to modify your _____.
8. Becoming a doer of the Word will expedite your _____ _____.
9. Your _____ always plays a major part in every victory you experience.
10. The very fact that you have made it this far in *The Victory Book* proves that you are _____ _____ _____.

11. ". . . whosoever shall say . . . and shall not doubt . . . but shall believe . . . shall have _____ _____ _____." Mark 11:23

12. Saying you are going to do a thing is a big step toward _____ it.

13. According to Joshua 1:8, when you meditate on God's Word day and night, "thou shalt make thy way _____ and then thou shalt have good _____."

14. According to Isaiah 48:17, it is God "which teacheth thee to _____."

15. Psalm 35:27 says the Lord has "pleasure in the _____ of his servant."

16. "The blessing of the Lord, it maketh_____ and he addeth no _____ with it." Proverbs 10:22

17. Second Peter 1:3 says God's divine power has "given unto us _____ things that pertain unto _____ and godliness . . . ."

18. John 10:10 says Jesus came that we might have "life, and that [we] might have it _____ _____."

19. ". . . this is the victory that overcometh the world, even our _____." 1 John 5:4

20. ". . . without _____ it is impossible to please him. . . ."Hebrews 11:6

21. ". . . If God be for us, who can be _____ us?" Romans 8:31

22. ". . . all things are possible to him that _____." Mark 9:23

23. ". . . According to your _____ be it unto you." Matthew 9:29

Answers: 1) behavior modification 2) your mind 3) transformed, renewing 4) doer 5) hearing, Word 6) hoped 7) behavior 8) financial freedom 9) will 10) willing to change 11) whatsoever he saith 12) doing 13) prosperous, success 14) profit 15) prosperity 16) rich, sorrow 17) all, life 18) more abundantly 19) faith 20) faith 21) against 22) believeth 23) faith

7

Phase I — Generating Cash Flow

We designed this chapter to help you raise additional cash. If you happen to be one of those people whose payments are more than your income, the strategies in this chapter may help you overcome your seemingly impossible situation. If you already have a balanced budget, you should use the extra cash you generate to pay off a portion of your existing debt.

These Are Proven Methods

These strategies are not just some new ideas that we're trying out on you. They are proven methods that have helped people just like you. Even if some of the suggestions do not appeal to you at first, please do not ignore them. Remember, it was doing only the things that appealed to you that contributed to your present debt problem.

Section A
Use It Or Sell It

With the following information, you should be able to produce some extra money. Hopefully it will be enough to prepay at least one of your bills. The first method we will discuss is selling some of the things you no longer need. Don't make the mistake of supposing that you have nothing to sell. It will surprise you how much money you can raise on just a few surplus items.

Give It Some Thought

Let's think about it. After you bought your child that new ten-speed for Christmas, what did you do with his old bike? Is it still stored away somewhere just collecting dust? How about the two toasters you received as wedding gifts? Do you still have one of them boxed up in a cupboard? What about the boxes full of "stuff" that you never bothered to unpack after the last move? Don't forget clothing. Almost everyone has surplus clothing — especially items that the children have outgrown.

Every day people just like you are getting extra cash by selling things they no longer use. You can do the same thing by selling your surplus goods. However, so that you won't miss some saleable item, or worse than that, sell something you still need, you must carefully decide what you have that you can actually live without.

What Do You Own?

The "Things I Own" victory sheet will help you make an accurate inventory of your surplus assets. We emphasize that you must be thorough. Then you must sell any item you no longer use or that you can easily do without.

Things You Don't Want To Keep

Start your list with the things you are certain you **do not want to keep.** If you still owe money on any of them, **be careful to review the loan agreement** to be sure you can legally sell them before you have paid for them in full.

Things You Could Live Without

The next things you should add to the list are **those items you use but could live without.** For instance, if a second car is a convenience but not a necessity, you might sell it now and replace it later when you are debt free.

Things You Want To Keep

Finally, list the things you do not use, **but would really like to keep.** Use this simple test from chapter 2 of *Rapid Debt-Reduction Strategies* to determine if such an item should be sold or kept:
1. Do I really want to sell the item?
2. Will I enjoy having the item more than I will enjoy paying off the portion of debt that its sale would accomplish?
3. Will the item become of greater value to me during the months ahead?

Now proceed with making your list on the "Things I Own" victory sheet on the following page. Once your list is complete, you will be ready to tackle the "Things I Must Sell" victory sheet that follows it.*

---

* *For helpful hints on how to have a successful garage sale or how to write a classified advertisement, see chapters 25 and 26 of Rapid Debt-Reduction Strategies, Financial Freedom Series, Volume II. HIS Publishing Company, Hurst, TX 76053.*

Things I Own

(Check "Loan" if item is not paid off. Check "No" if item is not needed. Check "Need" if item is needed. Check "Want" if item is not needed, but wanted. Check "Sell" if item is to be sold.)

Item	Cost	Loan	No	Need	Want	Present Value	Sell

Things I Own

(Check "Loan" if item is not paid off. Check "No" if item is not needed. Check "Need" if item is needed. Check "Want" if item is not needed, but wanted. Check "Sell" if item is to be sold.)

Item	Cost	Loan	No	Need	Want	Present Value	Sell

Things I Must Sell

Item	Original Cost	Desired Selling Price

Things I Must Sell

Item	Original Cost	Desired Selling Price

Use This Valuable Resource

Do not let the information you have compiled on these forms go to waste. Use it to help you sell the things you no longer need. Their sale will generate the additional cash you need for accelerating the payoff of one or more of your debts.

Don't waste a penny of the money you raise. It is not for eating out or going to the movies. You must use it to bring your overspent budget back into balance. **Whatever you do, don't forget that portion of your increase that belongs to God** (the tithe). You must be faithful in tithing to keep the windows of heaven open over your finances.

Section B
Cutting Costs

Cutting back on the amount of money you spend can have a big impact on your out-of-debt plan. To help you understand where you may be overspending, you will be comparing your expenses to those of the average person (not to those of The Sample Family). Remember, average figures are just that — averages. They are meant to be used only as guidelines to help you get started.

If you remember, your "Monthly Expenses #1" victory sheet from chapter 5 had an area for listing the category of each expense. Look at that victory sheet again, page 85. On a separate sheet of paper, add the total amount you spend per category. That means adding together all items that are in Category A, then adding together all items that are in Category B, and so on, until you have gone through all the categories.

List the totals in Column 2 of the "Category Expenditures" victory sheet, page 107, which follows in this chapter. To find out the percentage of your income you spend each month on each category, divide Column 2 by Column 3. After doing that, you must compare that percentage to the average for that category by placing the difference between Column 4 and Column 5 in Column 6.

It's Really Not As Hard As It Sounds

If you feel confused, don't be. Look over The Sample Family example to help you understand how to complete your own "Category Expenditure" victory sheet. You will see that The Samples spend a total of $1,233.50 per month in the housing category.

They figured the percentage like this: 1,233.50 (Column 2) ÷ 5,000 (Column 3) = .25 (Column 3).

They are spending 25% of their monthly income on housing. This figure is right in line with the average. The Samples should carefully look at the categories where they are spending more than the average and see if they are able to reduce any of those expenses.

Keep in mind that you cannot reduce all categories. For instance, your mortgage may predetermine the amount you spend in the housing category.

After carefully studying The Sample Family's "Category Expenditure" victory sheet on the next page, fill out your own "Category Expenditure" form.

The Sample Family
Category Expenditure

1 Category	2 Total Cat. $	3 Mo. Income*	4 % of Mo. Income	5 Avg. %	6 Difference
A Housing	1,233.50	÷ 5,000.00	25	25	-0-
B Food	500.00	÷ 5,000.00	10	10	-0-
C Clothing	83.33	÷ 5,000.00	2	5	–3
D Medical	64.00	÷ 5,000.00	1	3	–2
E Transportation	126.32	÷ 5,000.00	2	4	–2
F Gifts/Donations	658.22	÷ 5,000.00	13	12	+1
G Recreation/Ent.	215.00	÷ 5,000.00	4	2	+2
H Personal/Household	83.33	÷ 5,000.00	2	4	–2
I Insurance	118.30	÷ 5,000.00	2	4	–2
J Withholding Taxes	735.00	÷ 5,000.00	15	22	–7
K Support/Child Care	-0-	÷ 5,000.00	-0-	5	–5
L Savings	-0-	÷ 5,000.00	-0-	2	–2
M Miscellaneous	383.00	÷ 5,000.00	8	2	+6
Total monthly pmts. from "How Much I Owe" victory sheet	1,050.00	÷ 5,000.00	21	-0-	+21
Totals	5,250.00		105	100	–5

The Sample Family is overspending their income by 5%, or $250 per mo.
* See "Average Monthly Income" Victory Sheet.

105

Category Expenditure

1 Category	2 Total Cat. $	3 Mo. Income*	4 % of Mo. Income	5 Avg. %	6 Difference
A Housing				25	
B Food				10	
C Clothing				5	
D Medical				3	
E Transportation				4	
F Gifts/Donations				12	
G Recreation/Ent.				2	
H Personal/Household				4	
I Insurance				4	
J Withholding Taxes				22	
K Support/Child Care				5	
L Savings				2	
M Miscellaneous				2	
Total monthly pmts. from "How Much I Owe" victory sheet				-0-	
Totals				100	

* See "Average Monthly Income" Victory Sheet.

Category Expenditure

1 Category	2 Total Cat. $	3 Mo. Income*	4 % of Mo. Income	5 Avg. %	6 Difference
A Housing				25	
B Food				10	
C Clothing				5	
D Medical				3	
E Transportation				4	
F Gifts/Donations				12	
G Recreation/Ent.				2	
H Personal/Household				4	
I Insurance				4	
J Withholding Taxes				22	
K Support/Child Care				5	
L Savings				2	
M Miscellaneous				2	
Total monthly pmts. from "How Much I Owe" victory sheet				-0-	
Totals				100	

* See "Average Monthly Income" Victory Sheet.

Deciding Where To Cut Back

As you may remember from chapter 5, The Sample Family found that they are overspending the amount of their income by $250 per month. It is clear that they must make some cutbacks in their expenses.

The Sample Family's "Category Expenditure" victory sheet, page 105, revealed that they are spending 21% of their income to make debt payments. They have used credit cards and time payments to make purchases in every category, and now the amount of their monthly payments makes it impossible for them to comply with the average percentages. In fact, a close look shows they have already cut back in almost every category just so that they will be able to pay their minimum debt payments. Fortunately, their situation is not hopeless.

Let's look at the categories where they are **spending more than the average** and see if they can do anything to cut back there. You will see that they are overspending in categories F, G, and M.

Notice that Category M is 6% more than the average. This seems extremely high, but a close examination of their "Monthly Expenses #1" victory sheet, page 83, reveals that they have chosen to send their children to Christian school. They spend the bulk of their miscellaneous expenses on school tuition and fees. They will not be able to reduce expenses in Category M unless they are willing to temporarily put their children in public school. (We believe that taking children out of Christian school should be only a last-resort solution.)

In Category F, Gifts and Donations, The Sample Family overspends by 1%. **This area is so critical to their victory that they should leave it alone.** In fact, in future months they will actually be increasing their giving. We will discuss the reason for the increase in chapter 8.

Recreation and Entertainment, Category G, shows overspending by 2%. This may indicate a trend toward impulse spending. The Sample Family will bring Category G down to the average and see an immediate increase in their cash flow of about $100 ($5000 × .02 = $100). They will accomplish this by dining out less often and planning less expensive vacations until they are debt free.

How To Cut Back

There are many sources of information on ways to cut costs on everything from groceries to vacations. If you need suggestions on how to spend less, visit your public library or local bookstore for money-saving ideas.

The Sample Family's "Monthly Expenses #2" victory sheet on the following page shows where they have adjusted their spending to account for the $100 reduction they made in Category G. (We will deal with the remaining $150 per month of overspending in Section C.) After reviewing their form, choose which categories you will cut back in and complete your personal "Monthly Expenses #2" victory sheet.

We suggest that you write down each category you choose to cut back in, and list the methods or things you will do to accomplish those positive cutbacks.

Why do we call them positive cutbacks? Because you will see a reduction in expense spending which is a **positive factor, helping you pay off your debts more quickly!**

The Sample Family Monthly Expenses #2

Item	Amt. Per Mo.	Category*
Tithes	500.00	F
Offerings	50.00	F
Withholding Tax	495.00	J
Social Security	240.00	J
Mortgage	850.00	A
Groceries	500.00	B
Electricity	75.00	A
Water	50.00	A
Gas	62.50	A
Telephone	45.00	A
Christian School Registration & Tuition	350.00	M
School Clothes	83.33	C
Prescriptions	9.00	D
Doctor Exams	25.00	D
Dental Insurance	30.00	D
Gasoline	80.00	E
Tires	11.67	E
Car Registration	8.30	E
Car Inspection	1.25	E
Christmas Gifts	83.33	F
Birthday Gifts	16.66	F
Anniversary Gifts	8.33	F
*Vacation	25.00	G
Movies	35.00	G
*Dining Out	55.00	G
Barber	30.00	H
Beauty Shop	10.00	H
Toiletries	25.00	H
Veterinarian	8.33	H
Dog Food	10.00	H
Car Insurance	83.30	I
Life Insurance	35.00	I
Soccer Club	33.00	M
Car Maintenance	25.00	E
Property Tax	98.00	A
Household Maintenance	53.00	A
Subtotal	4,100.00	
Total mo. pmts. from "How Much I Owe" sheet	1,050.00	
Total Monthly Expenses	$5,150.00	

*Indicates Reduced Expenses

Monthly Expenses #2

Item	Amt. Per Mo.	Category
Subtotal		
Total mo. pmts. from **"How Much I Owe"** sheet		
Total Monthly Expenses	$	

Monthly Expenses #2

Item	Amt. Per Mo.	Category
Subtotal		
Total mo. pmts. from **"How Much I Owe"** sheet		
Total Monthly Expenses	$	

Section C
Correcting Negative Cash Flow

We designed this section to help those who have adjusted their expenses as much as possible and still find themselves overspending their income. At this point you should have completed Section A and sold your surplus belongings. You should also have completed Section B by cutting your costs in every way you can.

You May Be Able To Skip This Section

If your income now covers your monthly expenses — even if it is barely enough to do so — **skip this section and go directly to the Certificate of Accomplishment at the end of this chapter.**

However, if you are like The Sample Family and still owe more in payments each month than you earn, this section will help you create a temporary budget that should bring your cash flow in line.

What Is Negative Cash Flow?

Negative cash flow simply means that what you spend each month is more than your income. In the case of The Sample Family, we saw that their income is $5,000, but their expenses are now $5,150. That means they are still overspending their income by $150 per month. Their negative cash flow amount is $150.

There is an old saying that fits well here. It goes like this. "If your **outgo** exceeds your **income,** it will be your **downfall.**

If you are experiencing negative cash flow, you must correct it before you can be successful in operating any debt-reduction plan. You must find a method to balance your expenses to your income.

Can Your Income Be Increased?

The first thing you should do if you find yourself in a negative cash flow situation is to begin thinking about the possibility of **increasing your income.** You may need to find a temporary part-time job. Perhaps you can perform some service for extra money such as housesitting, baby sitting, yard work, etc. There may be overtime available or extra work you can do at home in your spare time for your employer.

Explore every possible way you can to bring in extra money to supplement your budget.

Keep Looking For Ways To Cut Costs

You must also continue to look for any remaining excesses in your spending. Trim expenses to the nub until you are in a positive cash flow position—that is, until your income exceeds your expenses.

Percentage Adjustment

If you have done all those things we have suggested and are still unable to make all your monthly payments, **do not despair.** There is yet another strategy that might work for you. We call it "percentage adjustment." It is a method of figuring the monthly amount you can afford to pay on your bills, and then asking your lenders to reduce your monthly payments to that amount. (Keep in mind that you cannot reduce any monthly payment without first making arrangements to do so with your creditor.)

Figuring Percentages Is Not Hard

To figure the size payments you can afford, you must first determine what percentage of your current monthly payments you are able to pay. Don't let the word **percentage** frighten you. This is not going to be difficult.

See how The Sample Family followed a simple formula to find out what percentage of their payments they could actually afford to pay. Look over their example below. We will then lead you through the same formula, step by step.

The Sample Family

Step One:

1. They listed their "Average Monthly Income"	$ 5,000
2. They subtracted their normal, ongoing expenses determined from their "Monthly Expenses #2" victory sheet.	−4,100
3. This gave them their total available dollars for monthly payments	$ 900

Step Two:

4. They divided their total available dollars	$ 900
5. By their total minimum debt payments	÷1,050
6. This gave them their percentage adjustment figure	.86

Now we will walk you through this same simple procedure to figure the percentage adjustment of your payments. Follow these steps:

Step One:
1. List your income from your "Average Monthly Income"
   victory sheet here   _____
2. Subtract your normal, ongoing expenses from your
   "Monthly Expenses #2" victory sheet (the subtotal).   = _____
3. Your total available dollars for monthly
   payments equals   _____

Step Two:
4. Divide your total available dollars   _____
5. By your total minimum debt payments* from your
   "How Much I Owe "victory sheet   ÷ _____

6. Your percentage adjustment figure is   _____

Once you have determined what percentage of your total monthly payments you can actually afford to pay, you must try to reduce each monthly payment to that percentage. You will figure your new payment amount by multiplying the current payment times the percentage. That is: "current payment" × "percentage" = "new payment amount."

For example, The Sample Family calculated the amount of their new car payment like this: $220.00 (current payment) × 86% = $189.20 (new payment amount).

A review of the following example will show you how The Sample Family figured the new amount for each of their bills. After you have studied it, complete your own "Percentage Adjustment" victory sheet.

---

*   *Be sure to subtract the payment amount of any debt you have already paid off.*

The Sample Family

Percentage Adjustment

Bill	Current Pmt.	×	% Adj.	=	New Mo. Pmt.
Car	220	×	.86	=	189.20
Dept. Store #1	40	×	.86	=	34.40
Dept. Store #2	40	×	.86	=	34.40
Credit Union	210	×	.86	=	180.60
Visa #1	125	×	.86	=	107.50
Master Card	50	×	.86	=	43.00
Student Loan	30	×	.86	=	25.80
Visa #2	35	×	.86	=	30.10
Unsecured Note	125	×	.86	=	107.50
Orthodontist	100	×	.86	=	86.00
Finance Company	75	×	.86	=	64.50
Totals	1,050	×	.86	=	903.00

Percentage Adjustment

Bill	Current Pmt.	×	% Adj.	=	New Mo.Pmt.
		×		=	
		×		=	
		×		=	
		×		=	
		×		=	
		×		=	
		×		=	
		×		=	
		×		=	
		×		=	
		×		=	
		×		=	
		×		=	
		×		=	
		×		=	
		×		=	
		×		=	
		×		=	
		×		=	
		×		=	
		×		=	
		×		=	
		×		=	
		×		=	
		×		=	
		×		=	
		×		=	
		×		=	
		×		=	
		×		=	
Totals		×		=	

Percentage Adjustment

Bill	Current Pmt.	×	% Adj.	=	New Mo. Pmt.
		×		=	
		×		=	
		×		=	
		×		=	
		×		=	
		×		=	
		×		=	
		×		=	
		×		=	
		×		=	
		×		=	
		×		=	
		×		=	
		×		=	
		×		=	
		×		=	
		×		=	
		×		=	
		×		=	
		×		=	
		×		=	
		×		=	
		×		=	
		×		=	
		×		=	
		×		=	
		×		=	
		×		=	
		×		=	
		×		=	
		×		=	
		×		=	
Totals		×		=	

Don't Call Your Creditor Until Everything Is Ready

With this percentage adjustment plan in hand, you should courteously approach all your creditors to explain your problem. You should be ready to show them your past budget and the new budget you have made. Make it clear there is no way that you can pay the total monthly payment. Then ask them to lower your monthly payments that small amount it will take to comply with your ability to pay.

You Must Get Permission

Remember, before you can legally begin making lower monthly payments, you must get permission from your creditors. Try to meet with them in person if at all possible. You should obtain their permission to reduce your payments in written form. Be honest with them by letting them know exactly how you arrived at your new, lower, monthly payment plan. Let them see that you are not asking them to bear the whole weight of your cash-flow problem, but you are spreading it equally among all your creditors.

Each time you get one creditor to agree, the chance that the next creditor will say "yes" becomes greater. So, every time you speak to another creditor, let him know which ones have already agreed to your plan.

Most lenders will help people who are sincere about restructuring their debts. This is especially true if you can convince them that you will stick to your new payment plan until you pay your bills in full.

Be Sure

Be sure of your numbers when you ask them to accept the lower payment, for it will be much more difficult to get their agreement if you have to go back a second time and reduce your payments again.

Act Quickly Once An Agreement Is Made

Send the new payment amounts as soon as all your creditors agree. Observation shows that once they accept a lower payment amount, they are not likely to take any legal action against you as long as you keep making the new payment amount on time.

If Some Say "No"

Try your best to convince every lender to accept your new plan. However, if one will not agree, notify the other creditors that he will not cooperate and re-figure the amounts you will be able to pay each of them. If only one or two say "no," it will not take much adjustment on the part of those who have already agreed.

Faithfulness Will Pay Off

When you have established a payment schedule that fits your budget, faithfully pay that amount until your first debt is paid off. **That event is just what you have been working toward.** Once you have eliminated the first bill, you will be ready for the next chapter. You will then have the ammunition you need to activate **The Master Plan.**

Victory Is At Hand

When you have balanced your cash flow, you should feel a great sense of accomplishment. It is no small feat in this day and age to have sufficient income to cover your outgo.

If things appear to be **tight,** realize this situation is **only temporary.** In the coming months you will make great strides in your war on debt. Begin planning your victory celebration now. Complete the following sentence.

When we have paid off all our bills, we will_____
_____
_____

Fill in your name and the date on the following certificate. Put it in a place where you will see it often.

Certificate of Accomplishment

Positive Cash Flow

Congratulations are in order for _____!

You have completed Phase I of your out-of-debt plan and have balanced your expenses to your income.

You are almost at the mountaintop! From there it will be downhill!

_____
John Avanzini

_____
Patrick Ondrey

Date _____

8

Phase II — The Master Plan

With the information in this chapter, you will be able to launch an effective and rapid out-of-debt campaign. It will take you all the way to the financial freedom that few people have experienced.

From now on, you will be waging an offensive battle in your **war on debt.** One by one, you will pay off your bills. Each time you pay one, you can pay off the next one that much faster. Then, all of a sudden, the finish line will be before you, and you will join the ranks of the totally debt free.

Section A
Why Not Base Your Program On The Golden Rule?

We encourage you to make a quality decision at this time. Why not move your out-of-debt program beyond your own abilities? We are suggesting that you put a powerful biblical principle to work on your behalf — **the golden rule.** Yes, that's right. Why not do unto someone else that which you would like to happen to you?

> **... all things whatsoever ye would that men should do to you, do ye even so to them: for this is the law and the prophets.**
> **Matthew 7:12**

The golden rule is a basic biblical principle found throughout the Word of God. Whatever you cause to happen for someone else, God will cause that same thing to happen for you. Scripture is clear about it. You will reap what you have sown!

> **... whatsoever a man soweth, that shall he also reap.**
> **Galatians 6:7**

Getting out of debt is no exception to this rule. **If you help someone else get out of debt,** God will be faithful in helping you get out of debt. Read what the Word of God says:

> **... whatsoever good thing any man doeth, the same shall he receive of the Lord....**
>
> **Ephesians 6:8**

A Revolutionary Plan

Hold on to your hat, for we are about to share a revolutionary plan with you—a plan that will enable you to help someone else pay off his debts.

You may be saying, "Wait a minute! I thought *I* was going to get out of debt!" **You are**, but remember what you just read. Whatever you cause to happen for someone else, **God will cause that same thing to happen for you!** You can actually recruit the help of Jehovah God in getting yourself out of debt if you will help someone else out of debt.

The Choice Is Yours

Whoever you choose to help is up to you. You may want to help one of your children, another relative, or even better, **your church.** As you choose who you will bless with a seed toward his debt reduction, you will open the doorway through which God can bring your own **miracle of debt cancelation!** With a seed planted, a biblical basis is established for God to help speed you out of your debt problem.

According to the principles of biblical economics, you can reach financial freedom more quickly if you help someone else reach financial freedom.

Your Church Is A Good Place To Plant Seed

We suggest that you earnestly consider starting an out-of-debt campaign in your own local church. Wouldn't it be exciting to have your entire church family getting out of debt while they are paying the church corporation out of debt at the same time?*

Even if your church as a whole does not participate, you can still plant your out-of-debt seed there. Simply follow The Master Plan on your own. Whenever it is time for you to plant a seed, designate it for "Church Debt Reduction," and give it to your church.

---

*   *If this suggestion appeals to you, ask your pastor to contact His Image Ministries for further information, P. O. Box 1057, Hurst, TX 76053, 817-485-2962. Seminars are available as well as discounts on volume orders of **The Victory Book**.*

You may choose someone else or some ministry other than your local church in which to plant your out-of-debt seed. With each seed you plant, simply send a note explaining that the recipients are to apply the amount given to the payoff of their debts. (Just be sure you are planting in good ground.)

How Much Seed Should You Plant?

We suggest that as you pay off each of your bills, you commit 10 percent of the amount of its payment as a monthly seed to help someone else become debt free. If you do not want to seed to anyone, just ignore the preceding suggestions and go right on with The Master Plan.

One Last Time, An Open Heaven Is Necessary For Success

For this plan to be the most effective, you should be a faithful tither to your local church. If you are not tithing, the Bible says you are robbing God.

> **Will a man rob God? Yet ye have robbed me. But ye say, Wherein have we robbed thee? In tithes and offerings.**
> **Malachi 3:8**

The Bible goes on to say that **the windows of heaven are not open over the lives of non-tithers.** If you have come this far in this book and have not yet committed yourself to be a tither, please go back and read chapter 3 again.

Section B
Starting The Master Plan

You are now ready to start the most exciting part of your out-of-debt crusade. List your debts on the "Prioritized Debts" victory sheet **according to the number of payments that remain.** If this information is not printed on your most recent statements, contact your lenders and ask for it. Do not include your house or automobile at this time. You will continue to make the regular payments on them. We will deal with their rapid payoff in the next chapter.

The first bill you should list is the one that has the least number of remaining payments. Next list the one that has the second to the least remaining payments. Continue this process until you have listed all of your bills, ending with the one that has the greatest number of remaining payments.

On the following page you will find The Sample Family's "Prioritized Debts." After you have studied their list, you will be able to complete your own victory sheet.

The Sample Family
Prioritized Debts

Name	Balance	Min.Pmt.*	Interest	Mo. Left
Dept. Store #1	80	34.40	18	3
Unsecured Note	700	107.50	14	7
Student Loan	200	25.80	4	8
Orthodontist	1,000	86.00	0	12
Visa #1	1,500	107.50	21	14
Credit Union	3,000	180.60	12	17
Finance Company	1,200	64.50	15	19
Visa #2	650	30.10	20	22
Master Card	1,000	43.00	19	24
Dept. Store #2	2,000	34.40	20	59
Total Debt Payment		713.80		

These adjusted minimum payment amounts are from The Sample Family's "Percentage Adjustment" victory sheet.

Prioritized Debts

Name	Balance	Min. Pmt.	Interest	Mo. Left
Total Debt Payment				

Prioritized Debts

Name	Balance	Min. Pmt.	Interest	Mo. Left
Total Debt Payment				

Winning Your War On Debt

From now on, you must look at your debts as though they are one, big bill, and look at your combined debt payments as though they are one, big payment. Determine that you will continue to make that one, big payment faithfully every month until all the debts on your "Prioritized Debts" victory sheet are paid in full.

Your first goal is to pay off the debt with the least number of payments remaining, as quickly as possible. To do this, add any extra money you have available to its regular monthly payment. If you have cash from things you have sold, apply it to the payment also. (See "Use It Or Sell It," chapter 7.) If you have no extra money at this time, just continue to make your regular monthly payment until you have paid off that first bill.

When you have eliminated the first debt, you will have the special ammunition you need to work The Master Plan. At that time, you will apply 90% of the payment amount of that first debt to the next bill with the least number of remaining payments. The additional money added to the regular payment amount will cause the next bill to be paid off faster. You will give the remaining 10 percent of the payment amount to your church or whomever you have chosen to help.

How Seed Giving Works With The Master Plan

Look at The Sample Family's "Prioritized Debts" list again, page 131. Notice that the debt on their list with the fewest remaining payments is owed to Dept. Store #1. The Samples are going to make that payment until they have paid the bill in full. As soon as they have paid it off, they will have an extra $34.40 for The Master Plan.

The Sample Family will give 10 percent of that $34.40 — $3.44 — to their local church each month to help pay off the church debt. Then they will use the remaining $30.96 of the payment to help pay off the next bill on their list more quickly.

Once Dept. Store #1 is paid off, the Unsecured Note has the fewest remaining payments as well as a high monthly payment. The Sample Family will target it as the next debt for rapid payoff. With their additional amount of $30.96 added to the regular payment, they will pay off the Unsecured Note in six months instead of the seven months originally scheduled. After they have paid it, they will add 10 percent of that monthly payment amount to the seed they are planting in their local church — another $10.75. Now they are giving a seed of $14.19 per month. ($3.44 from Dept Store #1 + $10.75 from Unsecured Note = $14.19.)

Step By Step In Your Own Master Plan

Look at your "Prioritized Debts" victory sheet, page 133. What is the first debt you should pay off?_____

How many months remain until payoff?_____

Can you apply any extra cash to this first debt? _____ Yes _____ No

If so, how much? _____

Remember your commitment: You are going to finish the race! You are committed to attaining a goal! You are committed to being out of debt!

When you have paid off the first bill, how much (10 percent) will you have to help pay off someone else's debt? $_____

How much (90 percent) will you have for paying off your next bill? $_____

Be Faithful In Your Giving

As you follow The Master Plan, you will quickly begin to pay off your debts. Every time you pay off another bill, you will have more money to use toward paying off the next bill. Never forget to give 10 percent of that amount as a seed.

Help pay off someone else's debt, and you will move God's hand into your own debt situation. The more you give in this way, the more God will bless you in return. You will begin a cycle of giving and receiving like you have never known, and just see if God does not help you pay off your own debts in short order.

When you have paid the last bill on your "Prioritized Debts" victory sheet, don't stop giving. God will continue to bless your offerings by measuring more and more out to you through the open windows of heaven (Luke 6:38).

It is time to make another commitment. Complete the certificate on the following page and give a copy to your pastor or whomever you have decided to help.

Our Commitment To Help Someone Else Get Out Of Debt

This is to certify that we, the undersigned, have agreed to help the following church, ministry, or person get out of debt:

_____

As we pay off our own bills, we commit 10 percent of the payment amount as a seed. Each time we pay off another bill, we will add 10 percent of that payment amount to the amount we are already giving. We understand that as we help someone else out of debt, God will faithfully help us pay off our debts as well (Ephesians 6:8)!

_____
Signature

_____
Signature

Date_____

Our Commitment To Help Someone Else Get Out Of Debt

This is to certify that we, the undersigned, have agreed to help the following church, ministry, or person get out of debt:

_____

As we pay off our own bills, we commit 10 percent of the payment amount as a seed. Each time we pay off another bill, we will add 10 percent of that payment amount to the amount we are already giving. We understand that as we help someone else out of debt, God will faithfully help us pay off our debts as well (Ephesians 6:8)!

_____   _____
Signature   Signature

Date _____

Copy for Recipient Named Above

Careful Planning Is Needed

Now you must begin to organize The Master Plan for your debt payoff. Review the illustration on the following page. It shows how much of each payment The Sample Family will use as a get-out-of-debt seed, and how much they will use toward paying off the next debt more quickly.

Notice that they will not add anything extra to their student loan or orthodontist payments. The reason is that the student loan has only a **small monthly payment** and charges **a very small interest rate** — only 4 percent — and the orthodontist **does not charge any interest at all.*** The Sample Family wisely decided it would be more beneficial to continue making their regular monthly payments on those bills and add the extra money to their Visa #1 bill. This will shave off more dollars in interest and free up a larger payment to add to the next bill.

After you have studied The Sample Family's example, complete your own "Payoff Calculations" victory sheet.

---

*   *For further information on The Master Plan, see chapter 3 of **Rapid Debt-Reduction Strategies**, Financial Freedom Series, Volume II. HIS Publishing Company, Hurst, TX 76053.*

The Sample Family
Payoff Calculations

Name	Reg. Pmt.	+	Add'l Pmt.	=	New Pmt.	Seed 10%	Total (Cumulative) Seed	Add To Next Bill 90%	Total (Cumulative) For Next Bill
Dept. Store #1	34.40		-0-		34.40	3.44	3.44	30.96	30.96
Unsecured Note	107.50		30.96		138.46	10.75	14.19	96.75	127.71
*Student Loan	25.80		-0-		25.80	2.58	16.77	23.22	150.93
Visa #1	107.50		150.93		258.43	10.75	27.52	96.75	247.68
*Orthodontist	86.00		-0-		86.00	8.60	36.12	77.40	325.08
Credit Union	178.60		325.08		503.68	17.86	53.98	160.74	485.82
Finance Company	64.00		485.82		549.82	6.40	60.38	57.60	543.42
Master Card	43.00		543.42		586.42	4.30	64.68	38.70	582.12
Visa #2	30.10		582.12		612.22	3.01	67.69	27.09	609.21
Dept. Store #2	34.40		609.21		643.61	3.44	71.13	30.96	640.17**

* The Sample Family will maintain the regular payment schedule on these bills due to low interest rate and/or low monthly payment.

**The Sample Family will have $640.17 available to their budget when all these debts are paid.

Payoff Calculations

Name	Reg. Pmt.	+	Add'l Pmt.	=	New Pmt.	Seed 10%	Total (Cumulative) Seed	Add To Next Bill 90%	Total (Cumulative) For Next Bill

Payoff Calculations

Name	Reg. Pmt.	+	Add'l Pmt.	=	New Pmt.	Seed 10%	Total (Cumulative) Seed	Add To Next Bill 90%	Total (Cumulative) For Next Bill

   With the information from the "Payoff Calculations" victory sheet, The Sample Family has what they need to develop The Master Plan for rapid debt payoff. Study their example on the following page carefully.* We have provided several blank "Master Plan" victory sheets on which you will have the opportunity to develop your own Master Plan strategy. Notice how the dollars will add up as you pay off each debt.

   The Master Plan Can Work For You!

---

*   *To conserve space on The Sample Family's Master Plan, we have rounded off to whole dollar amounts. Because of that, the actual get-out-of-debt seed would be slightly lower. Also note that we have not figured interest , therefore actual time until payoff would vary slightly.*

The Sample Family
The Master Plan

Debt	Balance	1	2	3	4	5	6	7	8	9	10	11	12	13	14	15	16	17	18
Out-Of-Debt Seed					*4	4	4	**15	15	18	18	29	29	38	63	68	72	72	76
Dept. Store #1	80	35	35	10	-0-														
Unsecured Note	700	108	108	133	139	139	73	-0-											
***Student Loan	200	26	26	26	26	26	26	26	18	-0-									
Visa #1	1,500	108	108	108	108	108	174	236	244	259	47	-0-							
***Orthodontist	1,000	86	86	86	86	86	86	86	86	86	86	86	54	-0-					
Credit Union	3,000	179	179	179	179	179	179	179	179	179	391	427	459	112	-0-				
Finance Company	1,200	64	64	64	64	64	64	64	64	64	64	64	64	432	-0-				
Master Card	1,000	43	43	43	43	43	43	43	43	43	43	43	43	67	417	-0-			
Visa #2	650	31	31	31	31	31	31	31	31	31	31	31	31	31	200	47	-0-		
Dept. Store #2	2,000	35	35	35	35	35	35	35	35	35	35	35	35	35	35	600	643	267	-0-
Total in Monthly Payments		715	715	715	715	715	715	715	715	715	715	715	715	715	715	715	715	339	-0-

*In month 4, $35 becomes available for The Master Plan. The Sample Family will give $4 (10%) as a get-out-of-debt seed. They will add $31 to the Unsecured Note.

**In month 7, an additional $108 becomes available. The Sample Family then has a total of $15 for seed and $128 to add to the Visa #1.

***The Sample Family will maintain the regular payment schedule on these bills due to low interest rate and/or low monthly payment.

Within just one year and five months, The Sample Family can pay off every debt from their "Prioritized Debts" victory sheet! That is a time savings of three years and three months! They will continue to plant their out-of-debt seed each month and will still have over $600 extra to add to their budget.

The Master Plan
Year _____

Debt	Balance	1	2	3	4	5	6	7	8	9	10	11	12
Out-Of-Debt Seed													

The Master Plan
Year _____

Debt	Out-Of-Debt Seed	Balance	1	2	3	4	5	6	7	8	9	10	11	12

The Master Plan
Year _____

Debt	Balance	1	2	3	4	5	6	7	8	9	10	11	12
Out-Of-Debt Seed													

The Master Plan
Year _____

Debt	Balance	1	2	3	4	5	6	7	8	9	10	11	12
Out-Of-Debt Seed													

The Master Plan
Year _____

Debt	Balance	1	2	3	4	5	6	7	8	9	10	11	12
Out-Of-Debt Seed													

The Master Plan
Year _____

Debt	Balance	1	2	3	4	5	6	7	8	9	10	11	12
Out-Of-Debt Seed													

It Is No Longer A Dream

Using The Master Plan, how long will it take you to pay off all the bills from your "Prioritized Debts" victory sheet? _____

By now you are experiencing a new feeling of victory. Take a moment to look at your "Dream Budget" again, page 23. It is closer to reality than you ever imagined it could be. It has gone beyond a possibility. It is now a probability.

Update your plans for your victory celebration. How will you reward yourselves when you are totally debt free?_____
_____
_____

Compare what you have written with your previous celebration plans from page 20. You may be surprised at how your plans have changed now that you are coming out of the bondage of debt.

You deserve to be commended for your efforts. Write your name and the date on the following certificate. Keep it in a place where you will see it often.

Certificate of Accomplishment

Beginning The Master Plan

Congratulations are in order for _____!

You have successfully started Phase II of your out-of-debt plan. When you have carried it out to completion, you will be over the mountaintop.

It's all downhill from here!

John Avanzini

Patrick Ondrey

Date _____

9

Phase III — Automobile and Mortgage Payoff

Since you have paid off the bills from your "Prioritized Debts" victory sheet, you should now have a substantial amount of surplus money each month. It is time to adjust your budget to reflect your new, positive cash flow.

You will start by listing your expenses on the "Monthly Expenses #3" victory sheet. Remember when you first figured your monthly expenses? At that time you had to add a large figure that represented your monthly debt payments. This time you should need to add only your car payment.

Ninety percent of your old monthly debt payments should be uncommitted at this time. You must now allocate a portion of that 90 percent to some new and wonderful things.

First, decide how much you want to add to your giving. $_____ Then, decide how much you want to add to your savings account each month. $_____

If you cut back on funds for entertainment during the time you were paying off your debts, add an amount for that now. $_____

You may also notice that your diligence in watching your spending has resulted in your clothes, tires, or other necessities becoming a bit worn. Include something in your new budget to replace the needed items you have put off buying. $_____

Take a look at The Sample Family's "Monthly Expenses #3" victory sheet on the following page before you complete your own. Notice that they have added to their giving and can still afford to set money aside in a savings account. The only two debts they still owe are their mortgage and car payments. They even have money allocated for unexpected expenses — something they could never provide for before.

The Sample Family's monthly expenses were $5,250.00 when they began *The Victory Book*. They were overspending their income by $250.00 every month. Now their monthly expenses are only $4,689.20, even after adding some extras into their budget. They have a surplus of $310.00 to add to their car payment. With this additional amount, they will pay it off in a little more than one third the expected time.

After a careful study of The Sample Family's new monthly expenses on the next page, complete your "Monthly Expenses #3" victory sheet.

The Sample Family Monthly Expenses #3

Item	Amt. Per Mo.
Tithes	500.00
*Offerings	150.00
Withholding Tax	495.00
Social Security	240.00
Mortgage	850.00
Groceries	500.00
Electricity	75.00
Water	50.00
Gas	62.50
Telephone	45.00
Christian School Registration & Tuition	350.00
School Clothes	83.33
Prescriptions	9.00
Doctor Exams	25.00
Dental Insurance	30.00
Gasoline	80.00
Tires	11.67
Car Registration	8.30
Car Inspection	1.25
Christmas Gifts	83.33
Birthday Gifts	16.66
Anniversary Gifts	8.33
*Vacation	50.00
Movies	35.00
*Dining Out	130.00
Barber	30.00
Beauty Shop	10.00
Toiletries	25.00
Veterinarian	8.33
Dog Food	10.00
Car Insurance	83.30
Life Insurance	35.00
Soccer Club	33.00
Car Maintenance	25.00
Property Tax	98.00
Household Maintenance	53.00
*Car Payment	189.20
*Savings Account	100.00
*Unexpected Expenses	100.00
Total Monthly Expenses	$4,689.20

*Indicates change or addition to "Monthly Expenses #2

Monthly Expenses #3

Item	Amt. Per Mo.
Total Monthly Expenses	

Monthly Expenses #3

Item	Amt. Per Mo.
Total Monthly Expenses	

Section A
Car Payoff

Compare the total from your "Monthly Expenses #3" victory sheet to the total from your "Monthly Expenses #1" victory sheet, page 85. You should see a drastic change.

Our total from "Monthly Expenses #1" was $ _____

Our total from "Monthly Expenses #3" is   _____

That is a difference of $ _____

Our "Average Monthly Income" is $ _____

Our "Monthly Expenses #3" are   _____

Our surplus income is $ _____

How much of your surplus income will you add to your monthly car payment in order to rapidly pay it off? $ _____

Pay Cash For A New Car

By faithfully applying this additional amount to each monthly payment, you will pay off your car in short order. Then you can begin making provision for the time when you will need to replace your present vehicle.

To do that, you must continue to make the regular monthly payment, even after you have paid for the car in full. However, you will no longer make the ongoing payment to the loan company. You will now make it into a special, new-car savings account. Since you are already in the habit of making a car payment each month, it will be easy to set aside that amount for the purchase of your next vehicle.

Even if you need to replace your car before you have saved the total cost of a new one, this savings account will make a substantial down payment. That payment will cause the amount you have to borrow to be much smaller. With a smaller loan on your next car, you should pay it off more quickly. As soon as you have paid it off, you will have plenty of time to save enough to pay cash for the next car you need.*

---

*   *For suggestions on purchasing a new car, see Section V of **Rapid Debt-Reduction Strategies**, Financial Freedom Series, Volume II. HIS Publishing Company, Hurst, TX 76053.*

After they paid off their car, The Sample Family began putting $190 per month into a new-car savings account. The extra $310.00 they were paying toward their car payment then became surplus to them.

Section B
Mortgage Payoff

Once you have paid off your car, only one debt should remain — your mortgage. By using one or more rapid debt-reduction strategies, you will not have to spend the usual thirty years paying for your house. Furthermore, you can eliminate tens of thousands of dollars in interest cost.

You can choose from many strategies to rapidly pay off your house. You can use The First-Day Payment Strategy by making the first payment on your loan the day you close escrow. This will shave several months off the time it will take to pay off your mortgage. Another quick payoff method is The Split-Payment Strategy. With this plan, you make one-half your regular payment every fourteen days.*

The Sample Family decided to use the Unspecified Principal-Prepayment Strategy. That means they will be adding additional money to their regular mortgage payments. They are going to use the extra $310.00 they were paying toward their car payment to put this strategy into place. They will add that amount to their regular mortgage payment each month until they have paid it in full. This strategy will cut down the number of payments they will have to make by more than half. Their house will be free and clear in a little more than twelve years. **That is a time savings of almost eighteen years!**

Which strategy will you use to pay off your mortgage more rapidly?

Section C
World Evangelism

Now that you are well on the road to financial freedom, God has a special assignment for you. It is one of the reasons you were born again. The special project we refer to is **world evangelism.**

---

*   *These and other rapid mortgage payoff strategies are explained in Section III of **Rapid Debt-Reduction Strategies**, Financial Freedom Series, Volume II. HIS Publishing Company, Hurst, TX 76053.*

> **... Go ye [the born again] into all the world, and preach the gospel to every creature.**
>
> **Mark 16:15**

There over five billion people on planet earth. Imagine how many die each day without ever hearing once about the Lord and Savior, Jesus Christ! How little you have been able to do to share the gospel with them in the past, but thank God, **those days are over!**

We are at the end of the age, and a world of lost souls is ripe to harvest. Almost every day we hear that the doors of other nations are opening wide to the Word of God. The Berlin Wall has fallen. The Iron Curtain is opening. Africa is hungry for the gospel. We believe the Bamboo Curtain will fall soon. We are about to enter the greatest harvest of souls ever known, but make no mistake about it. We cannot accomplish that job without proper financing.

You Will Be Able To Help

God created The Master Plan to accomplish more than just paying off your debts. He has not given you this opportunity just to begin lavishing luxuries upon yourself. Yes, God wants to bless you and give you the good life. Remember, it is His nature to bless His children. However, He has called you to a higher purpose than just being blessed. He wants you to **be a blessing!**

> **And I will make of thee a great nation, and I will bless thee, and make thy name great;** *and thou shalt be a blessing*
> *... and in thee shall all families of the earth be blessed.*
> **Genesis 12:2,3**

The primary way for you to bless all the families of the earth is to make the gospel of Jesus Christ available to as many as possible. While you were overburdened by the responsibility of your debt, you could do little to help with this good work. You were the servant of the lender. Now that you have been released from the bondage of debt, you can become the servant of God without interference. It is now time for you to begin properly supporting world evangelism.

Hear what God is saying to you about your part in the Great Commission. On the following page you will find a commitment to world evangelism. Prayerfully consider what God would have you do. Then fill it out and give a copy to your pastor or ministry leader.

Our Commitment to World Evangelism

This is to certify that we, the undersigned, commit to do our part in the Great Commission. God has instructed us to go into all the world and preach the gospel to every creature. Today we agree to be obedient to that command.

We will faithfully help the following ministries spread the gospel each month:

_____

_____

As God continues to bless us with financial increase, we will faithfully increase the amount of our financial commitment to the end-time harvest of souls.

_____   _____
Signature   Signature

Date _____

Our Commitment to World Evangelism

This is to certify that we, the undersigned, commit to do our part in the Great Commission. God has instructed us to go into all the world and preach the gospel to every creature. Today we agree to be obedient to that command.

We will faithfully help the following ministries spread the gospel each month:

_____

_____

As God continues to bless us with financial increase, we will faithfully increase the amount of our financial commitment to the end-time harvest of souls.

_____   _____

Signature   *Signature*

Date _____

Copy for Pastor or Ministry Leader

10
The Victory

When you started out on this journey, it took great faith to picture the end result. Take a moment now to realize how much closer you are to your "Dream Budget" than you ever thought possible.

For months you have diligently followed the instructions in this workbook and have maintained your commitment to follow through to the end. You have faithfully put The Master Plan to work. You have paid off your bills, your car is debt free, and if you are not yet living in a mortgage-free home, you are well on the way.

If you had not made the commitment to complete this book, you might never have known the true blessings of God you are now experiencing. You would most likely still be fighting the day-to-day battle of how to make those endless debt payments.

However, since you are no longer fighting that battle, you need only one last item — your victory budget! If you have already paid off your mortgage, you should be seeing a substantial amount of surplus money each month. If you are still making house payments, plan your victory budget for both before and after you have paid it off.

It is our hope that you will always continue your firm commitment to world evangelism and help finance the end-time harvest until Jesus returns.

Reward Yourself

Keep this in mind also. The farmer always keeps a part of his harvest for himself. God expects you to give **generously** to the gospel, but He also wants you to have blessings for yourself. As long as you are obedient in your giving, God will see to it that you have "everything you need and more, so that there will not only **be enough for your own needs,** but **plenty** left over **to give joyfully to others."** (2 Corinthians 9:8 TLB)

Take a look at The Sample Family "Victory Budget." Notice that they have absolutely **no debt payments.** Everything they need they can now purchase with cash. As their income increases in the future, it will simply add to their discretionary spending.

It became The Sample Family's dream to be able to give as much to world evangelism as they used to give toward their one, big debt payment under The Master Plan. The Sample Family's "Dream Budget" has come to pass for them.

Keep in mind that The Sample Family is only an example. You should create your "Victory Budget" according to several factors such as your age, the size of your family, and your desired lifestyle. A married couple whose children are already self-supporting will not need a college savings account. Someone only a few years from retirement may need to set aside a larger amount in the retirement savings account. A family of eight may need to save more in their vacation fund than a family of two, and so on.

After reviewing The Sample Family's example on the next page, complete your own "Victory Budget." See how much of your dream has already come true.

The Sample Family
Victory Budget

Item	Amt. Per Mo.
Tithe	500.00
Out-Of-Debt Seed	82.50
Other Offerings	67.50
World Evangelism	715.00
Withholding Tax	495.00
Social Security	240.00
Regular Savings Account	100.00
New-Car Savings Account	190.00
Retirement Savings Account	100.00
College Education Savings Account	100.00
Christian School Tuition	350.00
Housing (Utilities, Property Tax, Maintenance, Etc.)	385.00
Food	500.00
Clothing	84.00
Medical (Exams, Prescriptions, Insurance, Etc.)	64.00
Transportation (Gasoline, Inspection, Maintenance, Etc.)	127.00
Gifts (Christmas, Birthdays, Anniversaries, Etc.)	109.00
Recreation (Vacations, Entertainment, Dining Out, Etc.)	215.00
Personal/Household (Barber, Pet Care, Toiletries, Etc.)	84.00
Insurance (Life, Car, Etc.)	119.00
Miscellaneous (Soccer Club, Etc.)	33.00
Discretionary Spending	340.00
Total Monthly Expenses	$5,000.00

The Sample Family's actual monthly expenses total:	3,275.00
Their monthly giving above the tithe is:	865.00
Their various savings accounts and discretionary income are:	860.00

Victory Budget

Item	Amt. Per Mo.
Total Monthly Expenses	$

Victory Budget

Item	Amt. Per Mo.
Total Monthly Expenses	$

Stay Out Of The Trap

Take a moment to reflect once again on how you got into that old debt mess in the first place. Do you remember how it happened? If not, review your answers in chapter 4 of this book.

Now notice how your spending habits and ideas about money have changed. How free you feel. At last you are able to be the true servant of your God!

Determine that you will never fall into the debt trap again. Make one last commitment — the commitment to remain debt free forever!

Let Us Know Of Your Success

Once you have signed the commitment to remain debt free on the following page, you will have completed *The Victory Book*. Please take a moment to let us know of your success. We would like to be a part of your victory celebration by sending you a gift. Complete the form below and mail it to:

John Avanzini & Patrick Ondrey
P. O. Box 1057
Hurst, TX 76053

- -

Dear Bro. John & Bro. Patrick,

We have finished the race by completing *The Victory Book* and would like to receive a free gift.

Please print neatly:

Name_____

Address_____

City_____State_____Zip_____

Date _____/_____/_____

Our Commitment To Remain Debt Free

This is to certify that we, the undersigned, solemnly commit to remain debt free.

We will never again allow ourselves to be comfortable with a lifestyle of debt. If at any time circumstances compel us to borrow for any reason, we will diligently apply ourselves to paying off what we owe in as short a time as possible.

We realize we have been able to accomplish this goal through God's love and grace, and we will continue to thank Him daily for the abundance He has given us.

_____
Signature

_____
Signature

Date _____

Our Commitment To Remain Debt Free

This is to certify that we, the undersigned, solemnly commit to remain debt free.

We will never again allow ourselves to be comfortable with a lifestyle of debt. If at any time circumstances compel us to borrow for any reason, we will diligently apply ourselves to paying off what we owe in as short a time as possible.

We realize we have been able to accomplish this goal through God's love and grace, and we will continue to thank Him daily for the abundance He has given us.

_____
Signature

_____
Signature

_____
Date

Copy for Pastor or Ministry Leader

About the Authors

John Avanzini was born in Paramaribo, Surinam, South America, in 1936. He was raised and educated in Texas, and received his doctorate in philosophy from Baptist Christian University, Shreveport, Louisiana. Dr. Avanzini now resides with his wife, Patricia, in Fort Worth, Texas, where he is the Director of His Image Ministries.

Dr. Avanzini's television program, Principles of Biblical Economics, is aired five times per day, seven days per week, by more than 550 television stations from coast to coast. He speaks nationally and internationally in conferences and seminars every week. His ministry is worldwide, and many of his vibrant teachings are now available in tape and book form.

Dr. Avanzini is an extraordinary teacher of the Word of God, bringing forth many of the present truths that God is using in these days to prepare the Body of Christ for His triumphant return.

Patrick Ondrey was born in San Antonio, Texas, in 1951. He grew up in Southern California and received his business degree from San Diego State University. After graduating, he held several key management positions with a worldwide retail chain. In 1981 he was appointed Chief Financial Officer for a major regional transportation company, and he eventually owned his own management and consulting business.

In 1978, Patrick accepted the Lord while attending the church pastored by John Avanzini at that time. He became a powerful testimony of how God moves in the life of the businessman.

Then the Lord changed the direction of his life, and in August of 1988, Patrick entered full-time ministry as John Avanzini's associate. He now helps organize Dr. Avanzini's meetings on biblical economics and conducts seminars on rapid debt reduction.

To share the testimony of your financial breakthrough,
you may write to John Avanzini and Patrick Ondrey in care of:

His Image Ministries
P. O. Box 1057
Hurst, Texas 76053

The School of Biblical Economics,
Home Edition

This powerful series contains
- *2 textbooks—*
  - * *Powerful Principles of Increase*
  - * *The Wealth of the World*
- *14 tapes—*
  - **The School of Biblical Economics,*
    a dynamic 8-tape series by John & Pat Avanzini.
  - **Giving, Receiving, and God's Abundance,*
    a 3-tape series of scriptures that will renew your mind.
  - **The Wealth Transfer System,*
    a 3-tape series containing an edited version of
    The Wealth of the World.

All this, plus a special study guide.
Total Retail Value of $140.00
You pay only $70.00

Moving The Hand Of God
Putting Memorial Prayer To Work For You

In this book John Avanzini takes you step by step, line upon line, and precept upon precept to learn a long-neglected biblical method of prayer that will not only focus God's attention on your need, but will help bring His speedy answer. Never again will you have to wonder if your request has been forgotten. You can do as many famous Bible characters have done, and turn your most urgent prayer into a memorial that will perpetually be positioned in God's sight, awaiting His reply.

$6.95

Package #1
2 Books: **Moving The Hand Of God;**
Powerful Principles Of Increase.
3-Tape Series: 377 scriptures on *Giving, Receiving, and God's Abundance.*
Retail value $40. You pay only **$30.**

Package #2
3 Books: **The Wealth of the World;**
Stolen Property Returned;
Paul's Thorn.
3-Tape Series: An edited version of *The Wealth of the World.*
Retail value $40. You pay only **$30.**

Package #3
3 Books: **Hundredfold;**
Always Abounding;
Birds, Roots, Weeds and the Good Ground.
3 Tapes: *Things that Close the Windows of Heaven;*
Quality Stewardship; How to Get God's Attention.
Retail value $40. You pay only **$30.**

Package #4
2 Books: **War On Debt;**
Faith Extenders.
3 Tapes: *War On Debt; The Warehouse of God's Abundance;*
Faith In God/Faith Of God.
Retail value $40. You pay only **$30.**

Package #5
5-Tape Series: **Believers' Breakthrough.**
Retail value $40. You pay only **$30.**

Special Offer   *Special Offer*   *Special Offer*

Own this complete, up-to-date Biblical Economics Library.
Everything on this page, *plus* a copy of
Rapid Debt-Reduction Strategies.
Total of **11 books** and **17 tapes.**
Retail value of $213. **You pay only $90.**

Order Form

Please complete this form and return it with your payment to:
HIS Publishing Co., P. O. Box 1096, Hurst, TX 76053

Qty	Description	Cost	Total
	Package #1 — Offer 3026	30.00	
	Package #2 — Offer 3021	30.00	
	Package #3 — Offer 3022	30.00	
	Package #4 — Offer 3023	30.00	
	Package #5 — Offer 3024	30.00	
	The Biblical Economics Library — Offer 3027	90.00	
	School of Biblical Economics	70.00	
	War On Debt, Volume I	7.95	
	Rapid Debt-Reduction Strategies, Volume II	12.95	
	The Victory Book, Volume III	14.95	
	Have A Good Report, Volume IV	12.95	
	Moving The Hand Of God	6.95	
	Personal, Computerized Master Plan	25.00	
	Victory Under An Open Heaven (Cassette Tape)	8.00	

Subtotal ____

Please add 8% to your subtotal for shipping & handling ____

Total ____

Please print to insure prompt and accurate delivery of your order.

Name_____

Address_____

City_____State_____Zip_____

Area Code & Phone_____

Make checks or money orders payable to **HIS Publishing Co.**
Phone orders, call **800-962-8337.**

Complete the following information for credit card orders.

Please charge my _____Visa _____Master Card

Account #_____Exp. Date_____/_____/_____

Signature_____